The Long March:
Exploring the Franklin Expedition

Written by
Benjamin A. Turner, Dr. Austin A. Mardon, & Catherine Mardon

Edited by
Jessica Jutras

Copyright © 2021 by Austin Mardon
All rights reserved. This book or any portion thereof may not be reproduced or used in any manner whatsoever without the express written permission of the publisher except for the use of brief quotations in a book review or scholarly journal.

Inuit Nunangat Map, 2018 (modified/altered); Reprinted with permission from Inuit Tapiriit Kanatami, 2021.

First Printing: 2021

Typeset and Cover Design by Kim Huynh

ISBN: 978-1-77369-668-3
EBook ISBN: 978-1-77369-669-0

Golden Meteorite Press
103 11919 82 St NW
Edmonton, AB T5B 2W3
www.goldenmeteoritepress.com

Table of Contents

Introduction 1
Chapter 1 The Northwest Passage 4
Chapter 2 Sir John Franklin 30
Chapter 3 Captain Francis Crozier 51
Chapter 4 Erebus and Terror 55
Chapter 5 Netsilik Inuit 60
Chapter 6 Franklin's Last Expedition 73
Chapter 7 The Search for Franklin 80
Chapter 8 Modern Analysis 97
Conclusion 110
Appendix I List of Northwest Passage Expeditions and Rescue Operations 112
Appendix II - Crew List *HMS Erebus* & *HMS Terror* 115
Appendix III - Inuit Nunangat Map 118
References 120

Introduction

The Franklin Expedition is a topic that has held public interest all over the world ever since its disappearance, whether that is counted as the last sighting by whalers in Sannirutiup Imavik (Baffin Bay) in 1845, or later when they failed to materialize in either the Pacific or back on the Atlantic side of North America. For many people the mystery proves to be a tantalizing and irresistible bait. While we will likely never have a detailed account of what transpired on the ships *HMS Erebus* and *HMS Terror*, and later on Kikertak (King William Island), an impressive body of knowledge has been compiled from the artifacts left behind by the expedition, and by the eyewitness accounts of the Netsilik Inuit who have thrived in the region for millenia. The irresistible mystery becomes more clear, a set of events more coherent, with every new discovery from the experiences of previous Inuit Nunangat (Arctic) explorers, of which there were many, or oral traditions of the Netsilik that are now being studied more closely, or the ongoing archaeological discoveries that are made as global warming makes the region more easily investigated.

In conducting the research for this book, a few key details were discovered that are not often discussed in the colloquial version of the story of Franklin and his crew. Two major patterns emerged that do a disservice to the story of the Franklin Expedition. The first is the context of the hunt for the Northwest Passage. There were literally dozens of attempts made from both the eastern and western ends of the passage, and the map was largely filled in by 1845 with just a handful of notable gaps; the task of Franklin was to navigate what had already been mapped so that the Royal Navy could at last claim to have secured the Passage. To provide the proper background information and context to review these events, this book will spend a significant amount of time discussing an important handful of the expeditions that preceded the final voyage of Sir John Franklin.

The second pattern that emerged in the research is an overwhelming eurocentric bend to the story, with most authors completely disregarding the Netsilik accounting of events. To be clear, this book tells the story with a eurocentric perspective but will attempt to demonstrate an appropriate level of respect for Inuit culture and traditions, and take their oral histories into account where possible as well. Authors do a disservice to both the Netsilik and their readers by not familiarizing themselves more thoroughly with the traditional lifestyle of the people who live and thrive in the territory where Franklin and his men died. Moreover, they consistently refer to the Inuit Nunangat (Arctic) as a barren wasteland that is unfit for human habitation. This is a falsehood, but one repeated often enough so as to be mistaken for fact. It is true that the Inuit Nunangat (Arctic) is an extremely challenging place for people to live, but the Netsilik and other Inuit subgroups have lived there uninterrupted for thousands of years; their cultures predate all of the major powers of Europe including the Roman Republic. Expeditions to both polar regions of our world that have incorporated traditional Inuit technology and teachings have been demonstrably more successful than those that have not; successfully travelling for thousands of kilometers over ice and rock in relatively short amounts of time, and with significantly lower human costs than similar expeditions that ignored traditional Indigenous knowledge.

It is unfortunate that the British Admiralty saw fit to send so many men to their deaths on successive expeditions in the Inuit Nunangat (Arctic) without learning the lessons available to them through the Indigenous peoples of the region. And more unfortunate still that these many expeditions upset the balance of the environments they travelled through, at great cost to the people who have lived in these places for so long. Unintentional consequences of the frenzy to find the Passage include the transmission of European diseases to local populations, and destabilizing the food chain triggering famines that took many lives.

This book will provide an overview of a host of key elements to the expedition including: previous attempts to find the Passage, the career of Sir John Franklin including his other experiences in the Inuit Nunangat (Arctic), the career of Captain Francis Crozier who took command of the expedition after the death of Franklin, the ships *HMS Erebus* and *HMS Terror* including their use in polar regions and specific alterations made to prepare them for their final voyage, the traditional way of life of the Netsilik people with special emphasis on their adaptations to their environment which inform their technology and modes of travel, a timeline of the expedition itself that has been pieced together over the last 150 years, an overview of the most important missions sent in search of Franklin and his men, and a brief discussion of what the more recent research tells us about the fate of the ships and crew. It is through combining these complicated factors that I believe a reasonable picture of what took place emerges. The details are often unpleasant, but as with any story of which a central theme is the human will to survive, there is inspiration to be found in the horrific. Stories of this nature are conflicting because while the drive for survival is familiar, the actions required are horrific and difficult to relate to. If the Franklin expedition is a mirror, many people will find themselves uncomfortable with what they see.

In recognition of the traditional territory of the Inuit people, this book will emphasize traditional Inuit location names wherever possible accompanied second by the colonial names. Many of these location names are provided by the Inuit Tapiriit Kanatami (ITK), and their map can be found at the end of this book as Annex III. ITK has graciously allowed the use of their map for the purposes of this book. Some of the location names are taken from Woodward (2015), and are spelled out phonetically. Additionally, in accordance with the ITK National Inuit Strategy on Research, this book will refer to traditional Inuit territories as the Inuit Nunangat instead of the North or the Arctic.

Chapter 1

The Northwest Passage

Rumours and speculation about the existence of a shorter route to India and China existed in the popular imagination of Europeans for centuries before the infamous Franklin Expedition, with theories ranging from the concept of an open Arctic sea, to a mysterious Arctic continent similar to Antarctica, or an ice-locked territory (Brandt, 2010). The reality of the Inuit Nunangat (Arctic) is one of an archipelago, dominated by sea ice and reefs, shoals, and other hazards, topped with a permanent ice feature of multi-year ice as hard as granite that stretches from the geographic north pole and down into the archipelago. For Royal Navy explorers in the 19th century it proved to be a maddening and unpredictable maze where luck had far more to do with success than skill or technology.

European powers, enchanted by the promise of untold riches to be found in India, sponsored numerous attempts to find the passage. All of those attempts found their technology was not up to the task of navigating the Inuit Nunangat (Arctic) waters, and many people died pursuing this prize in the centuries prior to Franklin's expedition. This book will focus on the most significant English attempts to find the passage in the first half of the 19th century in order to keep things relatively brief. Indeed, these were the expeditions that saw the most consistent effort and added the most ink on the map to that point.

The English felt that because they were the dominant seafaring power in the world, and in keeping with their long tradition of exploration, they were destined to find the passage. It should also be noted that their desire to find it presupposed that the passage existed at all, despite a complete lack of evidence to that end (Brandt, 2010). The public was fixated on the passage, believing that it existed and England would be the country to make the discovery, and many of the explorers to lead expeditions became national heroes achieving celebrity status, perhaps comparable to Neil Armstrong and Buzz Aldrin following their successful landing on the moon. The end of the Napoleonic Wars had triggered the rapid contraction of the Royal Navy and contributed to a widespread economic downturn in the United Kingdom. In such hard times a strong desire can form within government institutions to give something for people to pin their hopes on; the combination of national economic pain and a scarcity of assignments for Royal Navy officers culminated in a renewed push to find the passage in the early 19th century (Brandt, 2010).

There was pressure from naval officers to mount voyages. When not actively on duty, navy personnel were only given half pay. To make matters worse, when at sea their food and lodging were provided, but while not on active duty they had to find those things for themselves; off-duty officers had higher expenses and significantly reduced income to cover those things (Williams, 2003). Naturally, this caused a number of senior officers to dream up voyages and expeditions to keep themselves and their crews working.

Finally, there existed a fixation at the highest levels of the admiralty. John Barrow, the Second Secretary of the Admiralty, had a particular interest in the topic and became the most important ally to the cause from within the government. As Second Secretary (later given the new position of Permanent Secretary because he held the office for so many decades) he had enormous power to choose which assignments were funded and who would staff them (Brandt, 2010). Barrow was a particularly stubborn adherent to the idea that there was an open polar sea, believing that ice could not form at sea because of the motion of the water in combination with its salt content. If this were true, it would be possible to sail over the north pole and drop down into the Pacific through the Bering Strait. This route would reduce the length of a trip to Asia by a significant margin. Barrow thought that the way to this open polar sea was blocked by ice, but if a way could be found or made through the ice, the passage would be consistently safe and relatively easy to navigate. The open polar sea theory was first proposed scientifically by Joseph Moxon, hydrographer to King Charles II in the 17th century; his reasoning for the idea included the nuance that, even if ice could form on open water, it would melt in the summer months because that far north the sun doesn't set in the summer months, and constant exposure to sunlight would surely cause it to melt (Oxford Dictionary of National Biography, 2017). Barrow held these beliefs in his mind for decades despite evidence that piled up after his own explorers conducted numerous expeditions on Barrow's orders that consistently provided evidence to the contrary.

In 1818 Barrow sent two expeditions in search of the Northwest passage. The first was led by David Buchan, who would Captain HMS Dorothea, with a young Lieutenant John Franklin leading the smaller, slower vessel on the expedition, HMS Trent. The instructions given to Buchan were to sail to Spitzbergen (now Svalbard) and search for a way through the ice into the open polar sea (Traill, 1896). The second expedition to leave that year was led by John Ross on the HMS Isabella, and William Edward Parry on the HMS Alexander. Ross was sent to rediscover sites claimed by William Baffin in the 17th century, whose maps and written records had been lost (Ross, 1819). All voyages of this nature were sent with two ships, so that if one got in trouble it could be rescued by the other (Brandt, 2010). This is an important detail because it is easy to view the attempts for the passage through a modern lens as pure recklessness, but consistently sending multiple vessels demonstrates a strategy of risk mitigation by the Admiralty. This strategy would pay off later on an expedition led by William Edward Parry and again during the search efforts sent after Franklin and his crew disappeared. This redundancy saved dozens of lives during naval operations in the Inuit Nunangat.

Hazards of the Passage

The Inuit Nunangat (Arctic) is among the most extreme environments on Earth, a very challenging place for humans to survive and travel without significant flexibility to the environment. Chapter 5 will discuss how the Inuit, specifically the Netsilik, have lived in this environment for millenia (Balikci, 1989). The methodology and technology of the Netsilik would be employed later by European and other colonial explorers in the 19th and 20th centuries to great effect in both the northernmost and southernmost places of the globe, but for Franklin and his crew these methods were merely the superstitions of savage heathens. History has shown us that while the Netsilik have managed to not just survive, but thrive in that environment, European explorers including Franklin were entirely unprepared for the realities of the Inuit Nunangat (Arctic).

The hazards of the Inuit Nunangat (Arctic) are numerous, and far more dangerous to those unaware of and ill prepared for them. Perhaps the most obvious and varied of these hazards is the ice. It comes in many different forms. One common form is that of pack ice, also referred to as ice floes or the pack, that forms vast sheets 3 meters thick that could crush a ship at the waist if caught in the wrong spot, or tear through the sides with a glancing blow. Pack ice is not stationary because it floats on the surface, so it's movements can be unpredictable and are determined by water and wind currents. When different sheets collide it piles up often as high as 12 meters above the waterline. Ships frozen into the pack ice are carried with it, helpless against the motion until weather conspires to melt the ice and release the vessel. Ships caught in the pack can be forced up against coastlines or smashed to splinters on rocky cliffs. They can be crushed, broken at the waterline if multiple floes move in contrary directions, lifted up above the waterline if pressure builds below, or driven downwards if the pack applies pressure from above (Brandt, 2010).

There are also icebergs which float freely with 70% of their mass hidden under the water. These unpredictable bodies can flip over unexpectedly or break apart without warning. Sir John Ross (1819) once noted an iceberg that was grounded and immobile in the water despite the depth of that area having been over 200 meters; he described that iceberg as an absolute monster that it was prudent to avoid. Icebergs can sometimes lurk below and unexpectedly rise to the surface. These are referred to as growlers (Brandt, 2010), and doubtlessly give sailors in Inuit Nunangat (Arctic) waters nightmares.

The region is also prone to extreme shifts in weather including powerful winds that can tear through sails, snap lines, and push ships into ice formations and shorelines. When the weather is calm it is common for dense fog to form, which not only reduces visibility to only a few feet at times, but the fog has also been known to condense on ship surfaces forming ice. This poses significant challenges to the operation of vessels, and can also increase the probability of capsizing. If too much ice forms, the vessel becomes top-heavy and is at significant risk. Snow is likely to fall in all months of the year, and in the winter months blankets all surfaces to a considerable depth. Temperatures in the Inuit Nunangat (Arctic) during the years of the Franklin Expedition routinely dipped below -50 degrees Celsius, making hypothermia and frostbite an obvious threat. Sweat becomes a major problem for an expedition in these conditions as well because sailors working hard will sweat in their clothing, and when they stop moving the moisture rapidly freezes, reducing the insulating properties of their clothing (Brandt, 2010). The extreme low temperatures pose a different sort of danger as well. Crewmen working outside in those temperatures who move to indoor spaces, even ones kept cold by European standards of below 10 degrees, feel the rapid swing in temperature as unbearable. Doubtless the crews who overwintered on the ice were forced to develop some methodology for handling such complications, but this subject will not be developed to any significant degree.

A hazard not unique to the Inuit Nunangat (Arctic) but to sailors in general at this period was scurvy, which stems from a lack of ascorbic acid, or vitamin C. This is due to a severe vitamin C deficiency that causes symptoms including anemia, debility, exhaustion, spontaneous bleeding, pain in the limbs and joints, swelling in some places of the body, ulceration of the gums, gingivitis and loss of teeth. Many have described feeling as if broken glass had been poured into all of their joints and it becomes agony to move at all. It also causes scars from old wounds to open up as if they were new because scar tissue has to be constantly maintained as part of the normal body processes, but lacking proper nutrition the body is unable to maintain the scar tissue leading old wounds to open up again. There are psychological symptoms as well including depression that may affect decision making (DeSantis, 1993). Psychological symptoms could conceivably have played a role in the loss of the Franklin Expedition by compromising the capacity of leaders to think critically. A more detailed outline of the symptoms and causes of scurvy can be found in Chapter 8, but it is worth noting here because scurvy played an important role on all the expeditions discussed in this section, often playing the deciding role of exactly when commanders would choose to end their exploration and return home.

The lack of fresh meat and vegetables is a key cause of scurvy, which is naturally a problem on ships before advances such as refrigeration. It has also been observed definitively in the Royal Navy that sailors afflicted with scurvy who appeared to be beyond all help recovered rapidly once their diet was restored to a healthier balance. The Royal Navy had a great deal of experience with scurvy and had developed some tricks to combat it. First, it was common for vessels to procure fresh foods wherever possible from ports they visited. Hunting parties could also be sent out to catch fresh game. And bottled lemon juice was carried on Royal Navy vessels with a daily ration provided to each sailor to combat scurvy, although lemon juice loses its potency as an antiscorbutic after a period of time because vitamin C has a fairly short half-life. The best sources of the nutrient are fresh fruits and vegetables, but it can also be gained from fresh meat from most animals.

William Edward Parry devised his own unique solution for scurvy on his voyages. Travelling to the Inuit Nunangat (Arctic) meant that local game in significant enough quantities to feed an entire crew was often rare, ports of call nonexistent, and the very real possibility of spending 2 or more years in the region rendered lemon juice ineffective. Parry loaded his ships with mustard and cress seeds which he sprouted in his own cabin. It was the dead of winter in the Inuit Nunangat (Arctic) with no natural light, so the sprouts had no colour and would not grow into full-sized plants, but they did have nutritional value. Parry fed the sprouts to his sick men in the form of salads and their symptoms disappeared quickly (Parry, 1821).

The Hard Push: Expeditions from 1818 - 1837

John Barrow, Second Secretary of the Admiralty, advocated for and used Admiralty funds for two expeditions in 1818. David Buchan with the *HMS Dorothea* with John Franklin serving as second while captaining the *HMS Trent*, to attempt to sail north over the pole, taking advantage of what Barrow assumed was an open polar sea. John Ross led the second expedition, headed for Sannirutiup Imavik (Baffin Bay) aboard the *HMS Isabella* with William Edward Parry serving as Second aboard *HMS Alexander*. Both expeditions left London on 4 April, 1818 with massive fanfare (Brandt, 2010). The public was hungry for heroes and these men offered that.

Lieutenant John Franklin wrote to his sister, "It would be quite impossible for me to convey to you the amazing interest our little squadron has excited. Deptford has been covered with carriages and the ships with visitors every day since they were in a state to be seen." (Traill, 1896 pp. 56-57). The ships hadn't even left yet but already they were enjoying a degree of celebrity status.

David Buchan's mission to penetrate the ice near Spitzbergen was unsuccessful and plagued by hazards. It involved sailing along the edge of the pack searching for openings in the ice, referred to as leads, and sailing up those leads to see if they would take the ships through to open water. Again and again the crews guided their ships on this dangerous and often tedious work of sailing up the leads to find they bottomed out after some distance and were forced to turn around and return to open water. Often the wind did not cooperate with the direction of the leads and the expedition was forced to make its own propulsion with pure grit. One method is known as 'tracking', where on a narrow lead the crew disembarks the ship on either side of the ice and pulls it manually through the gap. Another method they employed is called 'warping', wherein ice anchors are driven into the pack ice deeply ahead on either side of the ship with long lines attached, the lines are wound around the capstan which was turned by the men to pull the ship forward; this technique could be used to break the ice ahead to extend a lead in some situations. Buchan's expedition was short-lived and did not add any knowledge of the Passage (Brandt, 2010). It's primary value, perhaps, was to give John Franklin some first hand experience commanding a ship north of the Arctic Circle in the vicinity of pack ice.

The expedition led by John Ross was far more noteworthy and included several important discoveries. As mentioned earlier, Ross left at the same time as Buchan. Their orders were to sail to Sannirutiup Imavik (Baffin Bay) and attempt to locate the entrance to the passage. If found, they were to sail through it, spending the winter in the Inuit Nunangat (Arctic) if necessary, and once they emerged on the Pacific side they were to sail to Hawaii (Ross, 1819).

Ross sailed to southern Kalaallit Nunaat (Greenland) to get up into Sannirutiup Imavik (Baffin Bay) on its eastern side, but found that what was usually open water was this time clogged up with icebergs and pack ice, and it turned out to be an uncharacteristically short summer even for the far north. Picking through Sannirutiup Imavik (Baffin Bay) in these conditions was risky and tedious work, characterized by short gains of a few kilometers when the wind cooperated followed by long periods, days even, where the crews were forced to sit and wait for the ice to clear out of their way. Ross was also forced to set his men about the gruelling work of tracking and warping his ships through the pack for hours on end on many occasions (Ross, 1819).

They continued in this fashion until, on 9 August 1818 in Melville Bay, they made first contact with a group of Inuit. Ross was fascinated by them and spent as much time as possible there, only leaving when forced to do so by favourable conditions of the ice. Every opportunity in the Inuit Nunangat (Arctic) must be seized. The impression they made on him was significant, however, causing Ross to devote an entire chapter of his published account to these extraordinary people. He dubbed them "Arctic Highlanders" (Ross, 1819), although the true name of this subgroup of Inuit is Inughuit (Appelt et al, 2014).

All Inuit groups are highly specialized to their specific region of the Inuit Nunangat (Arctic), and can be differentiated by the technologies they have developed or not based on need and available resources. Two of the most noteworthy points about the Inughuit when Ross met them are that they did not use kayaks (Ross 1819) although that is a common mode of transportation and hunting among other Inuit groups, and they had access to iron to make tools despite not maintaining trading relationships with outside communities (Ross, 1819). Their iron came from a rich deposit 40 km inland from an ancient meteorite (Appelt et al, 2014).

Ross was so enchanted by the Inughuit that he was criticized for the amount of time he devoted to interacting with them during the voyage, and then again with how much he wrote about them in his account of the expedition (Brandt, 2010). The Inughuit live near the northern tip of Sannirutiup Imavik (Baffin Bay), and when Ross left them he headed north. They came to a place Baffin named Smith Sound which is a body of water bracketed by Mirnguiqsirvik (Ellesmere Island) to the west and Kalaallit Nunaat (Greenland) to the east. The sound was full of ice and at the far end they could see a wall of ice that appeared impenetrable from more than 80 km away; Ross decided not to investigate further, turning south instead. This decision made some of the officers uneasy, with William Edward Parry, captain of the *Alexander*, wondering aloud why they were not investigating more thoroughly. Ross scolded Parry publicly for questioning his decisions and made it clear that he was not interested in feedback (Brandt, 2010).

Sailing south along the coast of Mirnguiqsirvik (Ellesmere Island), Ross passed by Jones Sound without investigating it either. This is actually a straight, dividing Mirnguiqsirvik (Ellesmere Island) from Tallurutit (Devon Island), but is generally closed by ice year-round at the narrow western end (Brandt, 2010).

On 29 August 1818, Ross reached Tallurutiup Imanga (Lancaster Sound), which was completely free of ice and decided to finally make a more thorough investigation. In his account, Ross (1819) claimed to have sailed nearly 130 km (80 miles) into Tallurutiup Imanga (Lancaster Sound). The ships were hounded by alternating poor weather conditions of rain, snow, and dense fog, making it very difficult to see where they were going. The *Isabella* was the faster ship on the expedition by far, with *Alexander* trailing several kilometers behind. According to Ross (1819), he was called up on deck because the fog had temporarily cleared and visibility improved. He wrote that he saw in the distance a mountain range blocking their path eight leagues (40 km) in the distance, and ice completely blocking them off barely a dozen kilometers ahead. He ordered the ships to be turned around. The account was disputed by other officers on board, but William Edward

Parry aboard the Alexander was too far behind to add any comment. Many speculated that the weather was too poor to have seen anything of consequence, others pointed out that Ross didn't have particularly good vision to begin with. One journalist in London remarked that nothing could have been seen so far off, although the cold air of the Inuit Nunangat (Arctic) is known to play strange tricks with the light; landscapes hundreds of kilometers away are sometimes viewed as though they are just over the next hill (Brandt, 2010).

It is impossible to know what went on in the mind of Ross in that moment, but whatever the reason he turned the ships around and spent the next few weeks further exploring Sannirutiup Imavik (Baffin Bay) before arriving back in London by November of 1818 (Ross, 1819). All told, Ross added a great deal of detail to the maps of Sannirutiup Imavik (Baffin Bay), excellent progress compared with the most recent attempts to explore the Tasiujarjuaq (Hudson Bay) in the mid to late 18th century. The public was thrilled to receive news and more detail about the Inuit Nunangat (Arctic), so publicly Ross was spared much criticism from the Admiralty. Behind closed doors and anonymous articles however, the Admiralty and many of his own crew were skeptical of Ross. They questioned his commitment to finding the Passage and implied that he didn't believe it existed and therefore was not the right man for the job. Many were particularly critical of his decision to turn around in Tallurutiup Imanga (Lancaster Sound), arguing that even if there was ice blocking the path he should have gotten closer and looked for leads (Brandt, 2010).

Perhaps he was simply bored with the experience. Picking his way through the ice at the southern end of Sannirutiup Imavik (Baffin Bay) was gruelling, tedious, and often dangerous work. The experience may have cemented the idea in his mind that even if there was a passage it would be useless, thus draining any enthusiasm he may have had for the mission. At any rate, Ross would not receive another command from the Admiralty in his lifetime, and would retire on half-pay to his estate in Scotland (Brandt, 2010).

A lasting effect of the decisions made by Ross in 1818 was to make future explorers paranoid about being accused of not searching hard enough. Every sound, bay, and cove would be thoroughly investigated from here on, sometimes at great expense in human terms as well as supplies and time. Nobody wanted to be accused of being less than totally committed to the task. This expedition would be a permanent stain on the professional career of Ross, but Parry would find in it opportunity; by June of 1819,

Parry was already picking his way through the ice of Sannirutiup Imavik (Baffin Bay) headed for Tallurutiup Imanga (Lancaster Sound) to finish the job that he and Ross started the previous year (Brandt, 2010). Parry was now one of the most experienced and famous explorers in the Royal Navy, and would become among the leadership of the Admiralty and the media as the most likely to complete the passage.

The public in England was obsessed with the search for the Passage. Sir John Barrow, the Second Secretary of the Admiralty, seized on that enthusiasm by planning two additional expeditions to proceed almost immediately. He had a daring plan, he sent one expedition by land through the Canadian north to the mouth of the Coppermine River where it meets the Ikiuqtaqtuup Imavinga (Arctic Ocean) at the northeast corner of the current Canadian Territory of Nunavut, with instructions to follow the coast east back to Tasiujarjuaq (Hudson Bay). For this mission he chose Lieutenant John Franklin who had served as Second in Command on the Buchan expedition a year earlier.

The second expedition would go by sea, through Tallurutiup Imanga (Lancaster Sound) to continue west because Barrow speculated that Tallurutiup Imanga (Lancaster Sound) was actually a strait. To lead this mission he tapped William Edward Parry (who went by Edward Parry), who had served as Second on the Ross expedition from the year before. Barrow was wildly optimistic in his vision, hoping that the two parties may even meet somewhere in the middle and complete the passage together. Or, failing that, they could at least build cairns for each other on the coastline and share information that way (Brandt, 2010).

Barrow tapped Franklin to lead the land expedition most likely because Franklin was a talented officer and quite charming, although nothing in his naval record specifically qualified him to lead an overland expedition to such difficult terrain. But Barrow was a stubborn man, and by the time of Franklin's final expedition in 1845 he would have sent dozens of ill-prepared expeditions to seek the Passage (Brandt, 2010). In truth, there was no naval officer alive who was both well qualified and in good enough physical condition to attempt an expedition to the Inuit Nunangat (Arctic) overland. Barrow appears to have believed that naval officers were capable of facing any challenge without worry, and did not entertain the notion that a lifetime of naval service was not adequate preparation to navigate the Inuit Nunangat (Arctic) by canoe and on foot with only the supplies a party could carry on their backs or hunt in the landscape. Franklin's land expeditions will be more thoroughly discussed in Chapter 2. For the purposes of this section I will just note that Franklin returned to England from this attempt in 1822, after 11 of the 20 men in his party died of starvation, murder, or simply disappeared (Brandt, 2010). His party had grown so hungry and desperate that they ate leather scraps off their uniforms, and there was also speculation that some may have survived by cannibalising their dead comrades. This is the expedition that gave Franklin his lifelong nickname, "the man who ate his boots" because he was forced to eat a pair of moccasins to survive. In the end, he lived by the generosity of the Dene people, who had travelled with him from his time on Great Slave Lake all the way up to the mouth of Coppermine River. They came to his rescue when one of his party members made a lengthy trek to find them and beg for aid. Franklin was rescued by the Dene who cared for him and the other survivors until they were strong enough to make the long trek back to York Factory, an HBC outpost on the west coast of the Tasiujarjuaq (Hudson Bay) (Franklin, 1995).

Franklin's first overland expedition was a disaster in its human cost, a fatality rate of 55% is an outlier in Royal Navy expeditions searching for the passage, outdone only by the 100% fatality rate of his 1845 expedition. But he did map a significant portion of the coastline, and successfully navigated birchbark canoes on saltwater in icy conditions (Franklin, 1995). Both of these accomplishments were significant, and the near total loss of his party won Franklin considerable sympathy with the public. Overnight, Franklin joined the ranks of celebrity explorers (Brandt, 2010).

Parry was a natural choice for the expedition to Tallurutiup Imanga (Lancaster Sound). He had been there before, he had proven himself a highly competent commander, and perhaps most importantly, he appeared to be more interested in thorough exploration and had been openly critical of the decisions made by John Ross in 1818 not to explore every sound they came across (Brandt, 2010). This made Parry and Barrow allies in the hunt for the Passage. He would sail on the *HMS Helca*, enlisting Matthew Liddon as Second aboard the *HMS Griper*.

Parry had clear instructions from Barrow: sail directly for Tallurutiup Imanga (Lancaster Sound) and determine whether it was truly a strait. By not wasting any of the valuable summer months investigating other leads, Parry arrived at Tallurutiup Imanga (Lancaster Sound) at the end of July, 1819, which was a full month earlier in the year than Ross did in 1818. Parry sailed all the way through Tallurutiup Imanga (Lancaster Sound), confirming that it was indeed a strait and had plenty of time and supplies left over to investigate what was to the west of Baffin Island (Parry, 1821). He found Tallurutiup Imanga (Lancaster Sound) to be nearly ice free most of the way, only turning south when they did encounter ice for the first time. He sailed nearly 200 km into Prince Regent Inlet, imagining it might connect with the Tasiujarjuaq (Hudson Bay), but was stopped by ice and returned to his westward exploration of Tallurutiup Imanga (Lancaster Sound). Parry continued west, keeping his ships on the same general latitude as Tallurutiup Imanga (Lancaster Sound), and ultimately reached as far as the 110th meridian, halfway to Bering Strait.

After passing that milestone, he reached as far as Cape Providence on the south shore of Ilulliq (Melville Island), but Parry encountered pack ice 12 meters thick (Parry, 1821). Impenetrable and solid as granite, there were no leads to be found. Parry was forced to drop anchor in the safety of a bay on September 5th, 1819. They were the first Royal Navy expedition to spend the winter in the Inuit Nunangat (Arctic). They spent 11 months locked in the ice before they were able to make their escape, arriving back in England at the end of October, 1820. Parry was immediately promoted to the rank of Commander (Parry, 1821).

By the time Franklin returned from his land expedition in October 1822, Parry was already midway through his second expedition to investigate the Tasiujarjuaq (Hudson Bay) as a possible entry point to the Northwest Passage aboard the ships *HMS Fury* and *HMS Helca*, with George F. Lyon serving as second (Parry, 1824). If the Passage was accessible through Tasiujarjuaq (Hudson Bay), it would have to exist on the coast somewhere north of Salliq (Southampton Island), which had not yet been fully explored by the Royal Navy. Parry picked his way through the Frozen Strait toward Iwillik (Repulse Bay), but it took weeks to cover the short distance due to dangerous ice conditions. He anchored his ships to large ice floes in hopes of being sheltered from the dangers of moving ice, but this method proved extremely risky. The floes could snap six inch ropes like cheap twine, and when bergs collided with floes they could break anchors weighing over a ton (Brandt, 2010).

Mindful of what happened to the reputations of explorers like John Ross, who were accused of not exploring thoroughly enough, Parry went to great lengths to map the coast of Iwillik (Repulse Bay). He was helped by the fact that once they reached it, the bay was free of ice so he could simply send boats up every inlet they encountered along the way to definitively show they were dead ends (Brandt, 2010). The plan was to map Iwillik (Repulse Bay), and barring any new discoveries to the Passage, to continue up the north coast of Tasiujarjuaq (Hudson Bay) and to find the point where the coastline of North America finally turns to the west (Parry, 1824). This location, wherever it might be, could reasonably be thought of as the southernmost entrance to the Passage. It was important to find an entrypoint as far south as possible because it might be assumed the climate would be more conducive to sailing than in Tallurutiup Imanga (Lancaster Sound) to the north.

By September of 1821, Parry had mapped Iwillik (Repulse Bay) and continued up the coast into more unmapped territory. It took the entire month to explore and map what the expedition named Lyon Inlet, after their second (Parry, 1824). In October the weather was turning definitively against them and Parry found a sheltered harbour on the coast of Winter Island where the ships would be safe from the fickle moods of the ice pack. They spent that winter interacting with a Netsilik group camped on the ice just a few kilometers from the ships (Parry, 1824).

Their long exposure to this group helped them build strong social relationships with one woman named Iligliuk, who provided valuable information about the geography to the north of Winter Island. She went so far as to draw a map, upon request, of the coastline. They first tested her by asking for a map of Repulse Bay and Lyon Inlet, which Iligliuk did with great accuracy. And then they asked for her to continue, to expand her map to the north, asking if there was a point where the coast turned westward. She drew a map of the coast, complete with inlets and bays, showing them an island where she said she was born, and then finally she came to a point where she showed them the coast turning west. There was land to the north, with a strait that opened up on a large open area of water to the west, precisely what they were hoping to find (Parry, 1824). Iligliuk's map was a ray of hope for these explorers, most of whom had participated in previous attempts and had become accustomed to the brutal reality of the Royal Navy approach where no information was taken for granted, and they were ultimately at the mercy of the ice. Knowledge of the geography was earned by a combination of back-breaking work and sheer luck. To have an Inuk woman map out exactly what they had set out for must have felt like a tremendous gift. In the depths of the Inuit Nunangat (Arctic) winter and after months of their ships being immobile, it likely gave the entire expedition a huge emotional lift. They knew exactly where they wanted to go when the ice released the ships.

On July 2nd, 1822, the ice let go and they were under way. The map drawn by Iligliuk saved them the tedious chore of fully mapping every inlet along the way, and they reached the strait she indicated at the end of the month. All progress halted, there was indeed a strait there but it was blocked entirely by a thick sheet of ice (Parry, 1824). They had no choice but to wait for it to melt and once more they were forced to stand still.

Parry used the time productively, sending out sledge parties to map the nearby inlets and the island to the north (which later turned out to be the western end of Qikiqtaaluk (Baffin Island)), interacting with the Inuit living nearby, and walking over the ice of the strait to a high point ahead of them. From that vantage point a few kilometers inside the strait they could see that to the west it opened up into a larger body of water, but it was covered with ice as far as the eye could see (Parry, 1824). After six weeks of waiting, the ice in the eastern half of the strait did finally break up. They sailed as far as they could into the strait only to find the ice in the western half still solid, affixed to the coast on both sides. They tried to break it up by ramming his ships into it, dropping weights from the bow, anything they could to force their way through. Nothing worked. By mid September it became urgent to find a sheltered place to tuck the ships away for the winter, and so they sailed east out of the strait where they had spent the last of the warm days of the year. They had named the place Fury and Helca Strait. Parry navigated the ships into Foxe Basin on Qikiqtaaluk (Baffin Island) to shelter them for the winter (Parry, 1824).

The plan was to take a risk next season. Stay through winter, then transfer supplies from *Helca* to *Fury* and send *Helca* back home to England, stretching one last season out of Fury without the support of a second ship in the event of trouble. Parry was certain he had found the Passage, if this strait could just open up for him. In the end, by July of 1823 when the ice melted, both ships were forced to return to England. Scurvy had begun to present in the crew and officers despite Parry's mustard and cress sprout salads and the fresh meat purchased from the Inuit. They were exhausted from 2 years of navigating and carving their way through the ice. And by August Fury and Helca Strait remained just as solidly frozen as it had been the year before (Parry, 1824). If this was the passage, it was closed by ice to sailing vessels, and their way through must be elsewhere.

It was a lucky decision, in any case, because Fury and Helca Strait actually opens on Prince Regent Inlet, which Parry had explored on his previous expedition. It was blocked off to the west by the peninsula they had named

Boothia, and the only way through was north back up to Tallurutiup Imanga (Lancaster Sound). This was unknown to all of them at the time, however, and it was a shared speculation of Barrow and Parry that Prince Regent Inlet featured a strait somewhere on its western shores that would allow access to the Ukiuqtaqtuup Imavinga (Arctic Ocean). The feeling was that if Prince Regent Inlet could be navigated, the speculated western strait would prove to be a reliable northwest passage. There was no logical reason to think this to be the case, it was pure speculation (Brandt, 2010). It is worth noting here as well that the furthest west Parry made it on this expedition was Helca and Fury Strait, and Franklin's furthest east on his expedition in 1820 was Point Turnigain to the west. The distance between these two locations in a straight line amounts to around 725 km (Franklin, 1995. Parry, 1824); Barrow's vision of the two parties meeting in the middle, or at least leaving cairns for one another to find, proved to be a serious underestimation of just how difficult travel is in the Inuit Nunangat by traditional European methods.

Barrow continued to push. He was pressing Franklin, who returned from his deadly overland expedition in late 1822, to begin planning another overland trek. Franklin, for his part, refused to rush the planning of his next attempt, having well learned the value of planning at the cost of 11 lives on his previous expedition (Brandt, 2010). Barrow put pressure on Parry to go back as soon as possible as well, which he agreed to do. This expedition was to go back to Prince Regent Inlet and attempt to find a strait at the southern end, as both Parry and Barrow believed existed. They both felt, however, that Fury and Helca Strait from the Tasiujarjuaq (Hudson Bay) was an unreliable entry point, and didn't want to see another expedition run out the clock waiting for the ice to open up; Parry would access Prince Regent Inlet from the north through Tallurutiup Imanga (Lancaster Sound). Parry made his preparations, this time commanding *HMS Fury* himself and giving *HMS Helca* to Commander Henry Hoppner (Parry, 1826). They sailed at the end of June, 1824.

The last time Parry crossed Sannirutiup Imavik (Baffin Bay) he charged right through the middle, picking through the floes and icebergs successfully and cutting his travel time to Tallurutiup Imanga (Lancaster Sound) by a month; other skippers, more cautiously, travelled north along the coast of Kalaallit Nunaat (Greenland), avoiding most of the ice, and cutting around at the end of the bay. Parry attempted his daring move of cutting through the middle again, but this time was sabotaged by the ice immediately. The expedition was forced to use every trick in the book, sawing, warping, and tracking the ships through (Parry, 1826). Progress was painfully slow and dangerous to boot. On August 1st *Helca* was nearly destroyed when one floe drove under the ship on one side while the floe on the other side slipped up above. The ship was turned nearly completely on its side. The vessel could easily have been crushed in such a scenario if the ice had been any thicker, or if the ship had not been reinforced for travel through the Inuit Nunangat (Arctic). Miraculously, the ice released *Helca* without any critical damage.

Ultimately, both ships were locked into the ice pack in Sannirutiup Imavik (Baffin Bay), trapped by the grip of the ice until September 9th. Parry (1826) recorded ice floes nearby standing more than 6 meters above the waterline, which means that ice extended more than 36 meters under the water. By the time the ice released them, sailing season was nearly over for the year. The start of September is usually when a crew needs to seriously start thinking about finding shelter for the winter, and avoid being captured by sea ice that moves, shifts, and has the power to smash a ship to matchsticks. On September 11th they reached Tallurutiup Imanga (Lancaster Sound), and shortly thereafter found the strait filled with young ice. To escape the grasp of the ice they used a technique referred to as "sallying," wherein the crew is all brought up on deck and lined up on one side, and all at once they run to the opposite rail repeatedly. The shift in weight rocks the ship back and forth, breaking the ice that has frozen to the hull and allowing them to continue (Brandt, 2010). This method is only useful for thin ice, but it bought them more time and allowed them to reach Prince Regent Inlet on September 26th, where they found a safe bay, Port Bowen, to sail into and allow the ship to be frozen in for the winter (Parry, 1826).

It was on July 20th, 1825, when they were able to finally escape the ice in Port Bowen. Immediately they set about searching for leads in the ice of Prince Regent Inlet that would allow them south, and they eventually found one on the western side of the inlet right against the coast. Parry sailed aggressively, hoping the wind would favour them and keep the ice off the shoreline. On July 30th the wind shifted, forcing *Fury* ashore briefly, but luckily did not cause much damage. Just two days later on August 1st the wind shifted again and forced both ships ashore (Parry, 1826). This time the damage was much worse. *Helca* came off alright, but *Fury* had substantial damage, and it had been forced up with such pressure as to be pushed on top of the fixed land ice. The stern post was broken as was the forefoot, the keel had been badly torn up. And when the wind shifted favourably again and both ships returned to the water, *Fury* was leaking faster than the pumps could push water out. Fury could go no further, they needed to attempt repairs (Brandt, 2010).

Before repairs could begin, they needed a safe harbour to shelter the vessels from the movements of the sea ice. They sailed in search but found no such space, and had to invent one instead. They anchored the ships among a group of small icebergs near the shore, blocking off the area with heavy lines stretched across the water; ice would run into and be deflected by the lines. Then they needed to make sure their icebergs didn't move, so they anchored those directly to the shore. Once the ships were safe, they were free to begin unloading the stores from *Fury* to the shore of Kuuganajuk (Somerset Island); it was a complicated undertaking. It involved moving everything from the ship onto ships boats and ferrying the items to the shore, ton by ton (Brandt, 2010). Once the ship was empty, they could begin the process of properly assessing the damage and repairing it. To accomplish this, it was necessary to expose the keel. The only way to accomplish this was to tie heavy lines to the ship, attached at the other end to ice anchors, and using pure manpower they leveraged the ship up onto the ice and over on its side (Brandt, 2010). Once the keel was exposed to air it could be given a proper review. All told, this process took weeks to complete. It was a massive undertaking that was eating up every conceivable resource, from manpower, food, timber, but most precious of all was time. Summer in the Inuit Nunangat (Arctic) is short, and now they were forced to spend most of it trying to save a badly damaged ship. In the end there was nothing they could do, *Fury* was too badly damaged and it would have to be abandoned, along with all of the supplies they removed from the vessel and stacked neatly on the shore. They named this place Fury Beach.

Parry was looking at open waters to the south, but with two crews overloaded on one vessel, and no support ship to come to their aid in case of emergency, there was no choice but to turn north and return to England. On his third attempt, Parry had failed to make any new discoveries and was guilty of the most serious of sins in the Royal Navy: losing a ship. His expedition was back within a year, but Fury Beach would become an important resource and checkpoint for later expeditions.

Franklin's second overland expedition was far more successful than his first, owing to the lessons he had learned. A more detailed account of this expedition will be provided in Chapter 2, but a brief summary is warranted here. Barrow pressured Franklin to sail from England on the same day as Parry in 1824, but Franklin declined. He wanted a long lead time so he could collaborate with the HBC by mail, and make thorough preparations to hire English sailors in advance as well; he wanted to leave nothing to chance. Starting his preparations in 1823, Franklin intended to set off in early 1825. During the two years before he left the HBC to agree to build him a proper fort and have it stocked with supplies in advance. He wanted pemmican made well before his arrival, and to have supplies in front of him and behind him at every stage of his expedition. The HBC was concerned about Russian expansion into Alaska threatening their fur trade, so they had a vested interest in exploration this time and agreed immediately to all of his requests (Brandt, 2010).

Things went remarkably well, he sailed from England in February 1825. They travelled first to New York, not York Factory on Tasiujarjuaq (Hudson Bay). It was a deliberate choice that actually saved travel time despite adding kilometers to the distance between his starting point and the fort being built by the HBC because it was easier to travel from New York, to York (now Toronto), then up to Lake Winnipeg and north to Great Bear Lake. The choice was a good one, and the party made good time getting north. They also discovered that public enthusiasm for the northwest passage was not limited to the United Kingdom, Franklin and his men received a hero's welcome in New York with thousands meeting him at the pier. His first night in North America Franklin was the guest of honour at a formal dinner with some of the most prominent citizens of New York (Brandt, 2010).

The plan was to spend their first winter at the fort built by the HBC on Great Bear Lake, then travel down the Kuukpak (Mackenzie River) to the Inuit Nunangat (Arctic) coast and map it as far as they could to the west. There was an additional expedition under the leadership of John Richardson that travelled with them much of the way down the Kuukpak (Mackenzie River); their mission was to follow the coast as far as they could to the east (Brandt, 2010).

Overall, Franklin's second expedition overland was successful and largely uneventful. They encountered the Inuit, first in a large group of several hundred, and later in smaller groups. Their travel was challenging but also successful, they were able to move in fits and starts, with ice and fog occasionally hampering their efforts. The party got as far as Prudhoe Bay, Alaska, before finally being forced to turn back and make their way up the Kuukpak (Mackenzie River) again to Great Bear Lake (Franklin, 1983). There were no fatalities, no illness, no equipment mishaps; in other words, the expedition was productive, and although he had not been able to round the shoulder of Alaska and travel down the west coast of North America as he had hoped, this expedition was not characterized by disaster. They spent 1825 getting to Great Bear Lake, 1826 exploring the coast before returning to their fort, and returned to England in 1827.

Sir John Ross, whose career had been effectively ended by the Tallurutiup Imanga (Lancaster Sound) incident of 1818, had not been given a new command of any sort by the Admiralty in the time since. He was wealthy enough that Royal Navy half-pay was not a major difficulty to him, so he returned to his native Scotland and built an estate in Stranraer from which he could watch the ships come and go in the harbour (Brandt, 2010). But Ross was a naval officer, his desire was to be at sea. He also wanted another chance to discover the passage and petitioned the Admiralty multiple times for another command with no success. The navy had no interest in giving a second chance to a man who didn't take the opportunity seriously enough the first time.

Steam engine technology was becoming more common in the 1820's, and Ross was keeping up with the latest developments. He was certain that steam ships would be the future of the Royal Navy, and that steam power would play an important role in getting through the passage. He felt that wind-driven vessels simply did not possess the power to break through the ice, and they were also subject to the direction of the wind, but a steam ship could direct itself in any direction at any time. He felt strongly that more advanced technology was essential to operating in the waters of the Inuit Nunangat (Arctic) (Ross, 1994). But the navy ignored his suggestions to invest in steam power research, and denied his proposals for future expeditions. Ross realized that if he wanted to return to the Inuit Nunangat (Arctic), he would have to do it privately. So he began looking for a wealthy benefactor to fund his expedition.

His friend Felix Booth, manufacturer of Booth's Gin, agreed to fund the expedition but expressed a desire to remain anonymous. Booth had a reputation for philanthropy, but for unknown reasons did not want to receive any credit if the Passage were discovered because of his financing. Ross was happy to oblige, and used Booth's money to commission the construction of a steam ship he called *Victory*. This, he believed, would be the key to finally breaking through the ice. He planned to steam to Tallurutiup Imanga (Lancaster Sound), enter Prince Regent Inlet, and search for a strait somewhere south of Kuuganajuk (Somerset Island) near the north coast of the continent

(Brandt, 2010). It was the same mission that Parry had been attempting when he abandoned the *Fury*.

Ross was delayed because his steam engine needed constant repairs, and left a few months late in 1829. This caused another setback right away. He had contracted a whaling ship from Ireland to come along and act as his support vessel and carry extra supplies, but when they arrived late the other vessel refused to go. They were leaving too late in the season, the whalers were convinced the expedition was doomed to fail already (Brandt, 2010). But Ross disagreed, so he transferred what supplies he could from them and pressed on without the whalers.

The steam engine was a complicated and unreliable device. *Victory* still had masts and sails, but enjoyed the added benefit of steam driven paddles mounted on either side of the hull. The technology, as it turns out, was too new. When it was working, the steam engine could drive the ship at a speed of just under 2 knots. What's worse, steam powered locomotion by paddlewheels on either side of the ship is not much use when battling the ice, the ideal vector for thrust is directly behind the vessel (Brandt, 2010).

Once underway, he made good progress under sail. Ross reached Tallurutiup Imanga (Lancaster Sound) on August 6th, entered Prince Regent Inlet and reached Fury Beach by August 12th. They saw no sign of the abandoned ship, but the supplies stacked on the shore were in excellent condition. The exception was the tents that were left there by Parry's crew; those had been shredded by wildlife. But the canned food was just as edible as the supplies he had brought along. They noted that the sail canvas was neatly folded and did not appear to have ever been wetted. And the shore was stacked with a wealth of coal as well, which was good news because they had been burning through their own supply to run the boilers and power *Victory*; they took 10 tons of coal from Fury Beach to top up their supply. Ross had been counting on this store of supplies at Fury Beach to make up for the supplies he lost when the whalers refused to come along so late in the season. The lower areas of *Victory* were occupied by the complicated machinery of the steam engine and there was precious little space for supplies. That was the main reason for hiring the whaling vessel in the first place. But here, on Fury Beach, they had access to everything they could possibly need and more. When they had fully restocked the ship, Ross noted that they had hardly diminished the stockpile at all (Ross, 1994).

They continued south but encountered a frustrating combination of ice and fog. They picked their way along the western coast of the inlet, just as Parry had, but with greater success. Through September they were able to make gains until they came across a mass of icebergs all pressed up against each other into one enormous, unstable mass. They could not go around it, and they dared not approach it. But the coast was beginning a westward trend here, and Ross thought it might be the entrance to a strait that could lead to the Ukiuqtaqtuup Imavinga (Arctic Ocean). They named the body of land they were tracking Boothia, after their patron. To keep *Victory* safe from the movements of the winter ice, they tucked into a sheltered place and named it Felix Harbour, again after their gin manufacturer patron (Ross, 1994).

The larger inlet which Ross thought might be a strait turned out to be a bay; he named it Bay of Boothia. This was the narrowest point on the peninsula of Boothia, just 27 km across. Over the winter, they sent out sledge parties to explore the surrounding territory, including across Boothia to the opposite coast where they finally reached the Ukiuqtaqtuup Imavinga (Arctic Ocean) north of Kikertak (King William Island) (Ross, 1994). It must have been a maddening realization. The Ukiuqtaqtuup Imavinga (Arctic Ocean) was right there, and they were separated from it by a 27 km strip of land.

The most significant discovery made on this expedition was by Sir John Ross's Second, his nephew James Ross. The younger Ross led many of the sledge parties that explored to the west, and was a capable naturalist in his own right. While exploring the west coast of the Boothia peninsula he came across the exact location of the magnetic north pole on June 1st, 1831 (Ross, 1994). Ross was the first to do so, and it marked an important scientific discovery. It was understood already that the magnetic north pole did not fall in the same location as the geographic north pole, and that the location of the magnetic pole shifted every year. The younger Ross was disappointed to find that there was no natural landmark at the location, so he had his party build a cairn at the site to mark the location. This decision met with some mockery back in England because by the next year the pole had drifted to a new location (Brandt, 2010), but it nevertheless made a suitable marker for the first human discovery of its exact location.

The younger Ross also explored and mapped the northern coast of Kikertak (King William Island), which he mistakenly believed to be attached to Boothia Peninsula by a land bridge. He named this feature King William Land (Brandt, 2010). He remarked at the time that wherever the Earth is blanketed in ice and snow, it was difficult to distinguish between sea and land. Moreover, the strait that he misidentified as land between Boothia and Kikertak (King William Island) is occupied by two smaller islands that further complicated his ability to distinguish land from sea. The confusion is understandable. Franklin's expedition would later walk along the same coastline of Kikertak (King William Island) on their journey south.

The elder Ross and his expedition spent the winter of 1829 in Felix Harbour, and the next winter just a few km's north in a different harbour, and the next winter just a few more north in yet another. They had managed to penetrate deeper into Prince Regent Inlet than anybody before them only to be trapped by ice that never seemed to melt enough to let them out again. They failed to discover a passage that would allow ships to cross Boothia, but the ice also would not allow them to travel back north to Tallurutiup Imanga (Lancaster Sound). The situation was quickly becoming dire, with supplies running low and the crew unable to free the ship from the ice. They were forced to endure a long trek on land, north to Fury Beach where there was food and supplies. Abandoning Victory was a hard decision, but they were beginning to starve and much of the crew was already sick with scurvy (Ross, 1994).

In April of 1832 they began ferrying supplies from *Victory* to the shore, and sledging the supplies on the long journey to Fury Beach where there was an ample supply of food to be had because after three winters trapped in the ice the party was running desperately low on their original stores. The other benefit of relocating to Fury Beach was that if they timed things well enough they could launch small boats into the Inlet and make their way to Tallurutiup Imanga (Lancaster Sound). The whaling fleet fished those waters in the summer months and the party stood a decent chance of being rescued (Brandt, 2010); it was their best chance.

The distance to Fury Beach was 290 km in a straight line, but the ice forced them to follow the shoreline closely. This increased the distance to nearly 500 km. To make matters worse, their supplies were too heavy to carry all in one trip, so they were forced to walk a distance, drop their supplies, and double back for what they had left behind (Ross, 1994). For much of the trip they had to double back for supplies multiple times, meaning they walked many more than 500 kilometers to get to Fury Beach. It took them until July 1st to reach their destination. Exhausted and starving, they feasted on what supplies were there. The boats left by *Fury* were in good condition, which was a lucky break. They decided to build a shelter from the spare timber and canvas so they could rest and recover their strength.

In August they started moving north using the boats in the narrow strip of open water between the coast and the still prominent pack ice that spanned the majority of the inlet, but when they reached Tallurutiup Imanga (Lancaster Sound), they found it frozen solid. They climbed the landscape to get a look around and could see only ice in every direction. There would be no rescue that year. The party was forced to return to Fury Beach and spend a fourth winter in the Inuit Nunangat, the longest of any expedition to date (Ross, 1994).

In July 1833, they had survived yet another winter and began to see the ice receding. The entire party was weaker, and scurvy was now present in every member of the party, although only a handful had died. They again headed north toward Tallurutiup Imanga (Lancaster Sound). They waited for weeks at Batty Bay for the ice to open up, and finally it did. On August 15th they were able to sail in their three small boats for Tallurutiup Imanga (Lancaster Sound) in a desperate attempt to seek rescue. They sailed along the shore next to Qikiqtaaluk (Baffin Island). When the wind failed, they propelled their boats with manpower by rowing. On August 26 they spotted a sail and tried their best to reach it, but the vessel had not seen them and was soon gone. They saw a second sail shortly and took chase, but it was too fast for them; only when the wind died down were they able to catch up by rowing their way to it. When they were picked up, both Ross's party and the rescuers were bewildered by an odd coincidence: the whaling vessel was the Isabella, formerly of the Royal Navy and the very ship Ross had commanded in 1818 when he first discovered Tallurutiup Imanga (Lancaster Sound). The ship's boat that was launched to meet them found the crew in a sorry state and assumed they were whalers that had come by bad fortune, and when Ross introduced himself he was promptly informed that was impossible, Sir John Ross had been dead for three years (Ross, 1994). They were saved, John Ross was back from the dead, and their return home sparked renewed public interest in the search for the Northwest Passage.

Even though Sir John Ross had mounted a private expedition, his long absence was noticed by the general public and the Admiralty. In response to public pressure, they opted to send an overland expedition to find him in early 1833. The most qualified officer to mount such a mission was Franklin, but he was in the middle of a different assignment at the time so they went with the next most qualified explorer: George Back, who had been with Franklin on both of his overland expeditions (Brandt, 2010).

The plan was simple: Back would take a lean crew of just three other men to New York and travel north just as Franklin had done in 1825. Two of those men were carpenters who could construct sturdy boats as necessary, and the third was a surgeon. On the way north they collected extra HBC men who were skilled at river travel and some volunteers from the Royal Artillery stationed in Montreal. Back knew that the most logical thing for Ross to do after spending so many winters on the ice would be to go to Fury Beach, so that was where Back intended to go.

He reached Great Slave Lake late in the summer of 1833. They intended to stay there for the winter and make their way to the northern continental shore near Boothia before travelling up Boothia to Fury Beach in the summer of 1834. Unknown to Back was that by the time his party had reached Fort Reliance on Great Slave Lake, Ross had already spent a winter at Fury Beach and was effecting a self-rescue in Tallurutiup Imanga (Lancaster Sound). Word of the rescue of Ross and the rest of his party from Victory reached Back and his party on April 25, 1834 (Back, 1836).

The Admiralty had prepared for such an eventuality, sending him with additional orders in case the rescue mission became unnecessary. Back was now to travel down and map Konajuk (Great Fish River) to the sea, and then fill in the blank space on the map between Point Turnigain and Fury and Helca Strait. The enormity of that task was apparently lost on the Admiralty, who expressed confidence in Back's ability to complete the task in one season despite all previous evidence demonstrating the difficulty of exploration in the Inuit Nunangat (Arctic) (Brandt, 2010). The change in mission parameters caused Back to change up his party as well, he had learned as well as Franklin the importance of keeping the party lean on such a journey. He dismissed many party members, reducing their total number to ten men. He also only ended up taking only one of his two boats downriver, and reduced the supplies they were to carry, keeping their burdens to a minimum (Back, 1836).

When his party reached the mouth of Konajuk (Great Fish River), they found that it emptied into an inlet of the Ukiuqtaqtuup Imavinga (Arctic Ocean) and it was jammed with ice. Back would name this place Chantrey Inlet. They climbed a hill to see farther and could see land to the north, this was Kikertak (King William Island), the Boothia Peninsula to the east, and a solid mass of ice extending to the west. His instructions were to proceed west to Point Turnigain and double back, mapping the coast as far east as he could. After spending some weeks waiting for the ice to melt, the ice to his northeast did clear, but it did not fit his orders. If Back had explored in that direction he would have found there was no strait at the bottom of Prince Regent Inlet, and also that Kikertak (King William Island) was an island, because James Ross had mistakenly assumed it was attached to Boothia (Brandt, 2010). Both pieces of information would have been extremely useful, but instead by August when the ice had not cleared to the west they returned to Fort Reliance for the winter and began the long trek home in February of 1835. Back's first command was generally considered a success, he had mapped the Konajuk (Great Fish River) in a season and hadn't met with any disaster along the way. He had also established that river as by far the most challenging of the major rivers to navigate in the region from the sheer number of falls and rapids along its length.

The last big leap in filling in the charts was made by the HBC, when the company decided it was in their interest to make a thorough map of the north coast of Canada. They sent a party of traders starting in 1836 to overwinter at Fort Chipewyan on Lake Athabasca. The group was led by Peter Warren Dease and Thomas Simpson. The summer of 1837 they successfully travelled down the Kuukpak (Mackenzie River) to the coast. They mapped all the way to Point Barrow, filling in the last 300 km gap on the charts of the coastline to the west (Brandt, 2010). It was at Fort Confidence on Great Bear Lake where the party spent the winter of 1837-38 before they would make their attempt to explore east with the goal of reaching Chantrey Inlet and exploring the west coast of Boothia.

The ice did not cooperate with these plans. The party travelled down the Coppermine River and traced Franklin's path east, but were blocked by ice before even reaching Point Turnigain, Franklin's farthest east. Smith walked ahead 160 km with a small party of men, past Point Turnigain and found a large gulf there that was free of ice. They named it Queen Maud Gulf, although the Inuit name for that place is Ugjulik, and walked back to the main party. Smith had grand ideas in his head about taking their boats to Ugjulik (Queen Maud Gulf) and exploring the open water, but was disappointed to find their boats still beset by ice (Brandt, 2010). It was late in the season, they had to turn back. Simpson was frustrated with Dease at this point, blaming him for their lack of success, accusing Dease of being too old and cautious to find success (Dease & Barr, 2002). They spent the winter of 1838-39 back at Fort Confidence.

On June 15th, 1839, they set out again. Down the Coppermine River to the coast and this time luck was with them. Ice did not block their path, they travelled a great distance and by mid August they had crossed the south shore of Kikertak (King William Island) and reached Chantrey Inlet, where they took a poll of the men over whether to continue. The party voted to carry on, so they sailed to the north and east up the coast of Boothia to settle the question of whether Boothia was an island or a peninsula. As they reached the end of Chantrey Inlet to the north, however, the weather turned and they changed their minds, they had been lucky and decided not to push it further. They returned to Fort Confidence (Dease & Barr, 2002). When they arrived back at the safety of the Fort, they found a letter granting them permission to take a year off at the much more comfortable accommodations on Great Slave Lake to the south, and they jumped at the opportunity.

Dease spent his time off getting married and taking a trip to England. Simpson kept busy planning another expedition and petitioning the HBC to give him lone command of a final push to locate the channel connecting the Gulf of Boothia to the Ukiuqtaqtuup Imavinga (Arctic Ocean) (Brandt, 2010). This channel, we now know, does not exist. But Simpson, Barrow, and the HBC were all convinced it was there. When he didn't hear back from the HBC, Simpson set out with the intention of sailing to London to confront the HBC board in person.

During this trip across the continent, there was an incident on June 14th, 1840, in which Simpson murdered his two Metis travel companions in a fit of rage. The rest of his travel companions fled in fear, returning the next day with reinforcements. They found Simpson in his bed, dead by a self-inflicted gunshot wound (Brandt, 2010). Unfortunately for Simpson, the day he began travelling to confront the HBC was the same day the board in London approved his request. Queen Victoria had also granted both Simpson and Dease a lifetime pension of £100 per year for their achievements. Dease opted to retire with the money and the HBC put their ambitions to discover the Passage on hold.

The advancements made by Simpson and Dease may not have settled the question of whether the Gulf of Boothia emptied into the Ukiuqtaqtuup Imavinga (Arctic Ocean), but there was now a reasonably complete map showing where vessels needed to sail to complete the passage. Many felt that the Northwest Passage had all but been discovered, the only thing that was left to do was actually sail a vessel through it. The next attempt would be made by Franklin sailing *HMS Erebus* with Capt Francis Crozier as his second, sailing *HMS Terror* in 1845.

Chapter 2
Sir John Franklin

Early Career

Franklin joined the navy at the age of 14 (Britannica, n.d.), which was a common practice in the 19th century. He soon saw combat, serving aboard *HMS Polyphemus* as part of Horatio Nelson's squadron where he saw combat for the first time at the Battle of Copenhagen in 1801. The battle is remembered as one of the fiercest naval battles of the Napoleonic Wars, with more than 1200 British sailors killed. Franklin was not injured, but he told a family member many years later that when he looked overboard into the clear shallows, he could see bodies littered all across the seafloor. For his first exploratory service, he served aboard *HMS Investigator* with Captain Matthew Flinders on his voyage to Australia from 1802-1803; under Flinders, Franklin served as a Midshipman, which was the lowest of the officer ranks. Flinders' expedition was an interesting event, they successfully circumnavigated Australia and definitively demonstrated it to be a continent, and not a group of islands. Franklin saw the Great Barrier Reef up close. At one point the expedition ran aground on a sandbar more than 300 km off the coast. The Captain took a six-oared ship's boat with 13 men towards Sydney, which was their only hope of rescue. Sydney was roughly 1300 km from where they were stranded, and the rest of the crew remained on the sandbar for six weeks until Flinders arrived with rescue (Brandt, 2010).

After returning to England from his first exploration service, Franklin spent a year on blockade duty off the coast of France aboard *HMS Bellerophon*. Blockade duty was, by definition, a dull affair. It was 1804 and Franklin was 18 years old. Excitement found him soon enough in October 1805. *Bellerophon* sailed with the rest of the fleet under Admiral Nelson to the Battle of Trafalgar, which was the defining battle of the Napoleonic Wars.

Bellerophon engaged in close combat with four French and Spanish vessels at once. They were so close their spars tangled with those of enemy vessels. Casualties were heavy, but once again Franklin survived almost unscathed. The only damage he suffered was the partial loss of his hearing from his close proximity to so much cannon fire. It was a low price compared to the majority of the crew, but it was a permanent injury (Brandt, 2010).

In 1807 Franklin was promoted to Lieutenant, very promising progress for a young officer. In the War of 1812 between England and the United States, Franklin saw action at the Battle of New Orleans where he was wounded in the shoulder. By the end of the war he had been promoted to 1st Lieutenant, and like most of the Royal Navy, was stood down from active duty and given a salary of half-pay (Brandt, 2010). Before his 30th birthday Franklin had served at the Battle of Copenhagen, Battle of Trafalgar, Battle of New Orleans, survived being marooned, and was injured in the line of duty. It was a shining record for a young naval officer, and may help account for why he continued to receive assignments from the Admiralty after the Napoleonic Wars had ended. The navy had been forced to make massive cuts, so there was no shortage of unemployed sailors to call upon. Nevertheless, in 1818 when Buchan made his attempt for the North Pole, Franklin was called upon to command *HMS Trent* and act as Buchan's Second. It indicates the significant promise his career must have shown to be called on to command a ship at that point in time

Land Expeditions for the Northwest Passage

1818 - First Overland Expedition

Franklin seemed to many an odd choice to lead the land expedition. He had no qualifications to plan and execute such an endeavour, and nobody would mistake him for being in peak physical condition; he was often described as corpulent. But Franklin was a charming man, also routinely described as being very nice. He had performed well on the Buchan expedition the year before, and he was enthusiastic about exploration (Brandt, 2010). Evidently, that was good enough for Barrow; Franklin would make the attempt to explore the North American northern coast on foot and by boat.

Most of the expeditions sent by the Admiralty were sea-borne, aboard relatively small, nimble ships with crews of maybe two to three dozen sailors. They were good at putting together these types of voyages, equipping them well, calculating the required supplies plus a margin of error, and coming up with clever ways to keep the ships warm and dry inside during the long winters. This wealth of experience did not exist for Franklin while he was planning his first overland expedition to Coppermine River. He was inexperienced at this sort of voyage, but he carried the habits of ocean travel with him. The people that could help him plan such a voyage properly, the Indigenous peoples, the French Voyageurs, to an extent the men of the Hudson Bay Company (HBC) and Northwest Trading Company (NWC), were all too far away from him to be of any use before the endeavour was already underway, though this was partly due to the limited amount of time Barrow had given Franklin to prepare before setting out. He had just a few months to plan an expedition that would be a first for the Royal Navy.

Prior to his departure, Franklin submitted a requisition list to Barrow that included: three hundred pounds preserved beef, two hundred pounds preserved mutton, a hogshead of rum (245 liters), a hundred pounds of portable soups, a hundred pounds of arrowroot, two hundred pounds of ships biscuits, a hundred pounds each of tea, coffee, and sugar, two hundred pounds of tobacco, scientific equipment related to the study of the Earth's magnetic field, several reams of paper, weapons and ammunition, surveying equipment, and scientific gear for the collection of plant and animal specimens (Franklin, 1995). A lifetime of naval service taught Franklin to pack everything he could possibly need, that he should enter the expedition with everything plus a margin for error. In different circumstances this is a prudent and reasonable course of action, and done easily enough when there is a sizable ship to carry you the entire way. In Inuit Nunangat (Arctic) travel, bulky ships are often too clumsy or run too far below the waterline to be successful. Overland travel is the more flexible option, but only when Inuit methodology is applied. This includes travelling extremely light, in relatively small groups of usually fewer than 20 people. Also important is food considerations; a party must be able to hunt and live off the land during their journey, carrying a bare minimum supply of reserve food, and an understanding that the party may need to go hungry for periods of time. And when long distances are to be covered, utilising dog teams to help haul the load wherever possible. Dog sleds speed up travel time and reduce the number of calories burned by the party members in transporting their equipment (Balikci, 1989). To plan an overland trek is wise, and sidesteps a lot of the hazards that face ocean-borne expeditions, but to plan to bring a large party with heavy boats and thousands of pounds of equipment is a dangerous proposition. The Netsilik are the Inuit subgroup who have lived in the region for many thousands of years. They have adapted to a lifestyle where no piece of technology they use is irreplaceable with locally-available materials. They also do not weigh themselves down with sentimental items, or anything that is not immediately necessary to their survival (Balikci, 1989). What the Netsilik understand is that calories are hard earned and easily burned in the Inuit Nunangat (Arctic), and wasting energy carrying extra weight is deadly. In their traditional lifestyle the Netsilik carry with them their tools for hunting and crafting, their clothing, and a few days of food at most. In the summer months they carry their sealskin tents that are light enough for a person or dog to carry on their own, and during winter travel they live in igloos and do not carry any shelter with them at all. English explorers in this time period on the other hand never gave up their heavy canvas tents; tents that were too bulky for an individual to transport, and that did a very poor job of keeping people warm in Inuit Nunangat (Arctic) conditions (Brandt, 2010). Franklin was doing precisely what he had been trained to do, but the price of those decisions would be very steep.

This expedition was also flawed in that it made a number of logistical assumptions. Franklin left London aboard a supply ship headed for the HBC trading post called York Factory on the west coast of Tasiujarjuaq (Hudson Bay). When Franklin departed England in May of 1819, he had just 5 men with him, assuming that he could hire more along the way, wanting to travel with a party of between 20 and 30 men in total. The ship made several stops on the British Isles before making the Atlantic crossing but Franklin was unable to hire the number of crew he hoped for, and when they finally did turn to the west he had attracted just another 4 men from north Scotland to come along; it was not an encouraging start. Franklin knew that to make up his numbers now he would be forced to rely on the HBC to supply him with additional men, as well as the canoes he needed to make his way inland, but when he reached York Factory there was more bad news. The HBC was in the midst of a brutal trade war with the NWC, and the rivalry between them was particularly ugly (Brandt, 2010). This reality would cause complications for Franklin throughout the expedition, but there was a deeper flaw in his plan to rely on the trading companies to supply him. He had assumed that because these trading companies worked for the crown, they would fully support his exploration and honour the chits he wrote on behalf of the admiralty, as was standard practice. But the HBC and NWC were businesses above all, and were not in the habit of stocking extra men and supplies at their outposts. Their purpose was to turn a profit and that meant lean operations without unnecessary bodies or food and equipment lying around (Brandt, 2010). They had very little to share with him.

York Factory gave him one guide and not canoes but a York boat, a river boat which is pointed at both ends. He now had a total crew of ten plus himself, one boat, thousands of pounds of equipment, and the distance to Coppermine River was nearly 1,200 km in a straight line (Franklin, 1823). It was urgent that he get underway immediately because summer in the north is short, and winter travel is nearly impossible for Europeans and even many of the Indigenous peoples. Franklin's goal was to reach Fort Chipewyan on Lake Athabasca that first year before turning north and descending the Coppermine River to its mouth the following summer.

Before Franklin could set out, he was forced to give up half of his supplies because they did not have enough men to help carry it all. The HBC promised to send the supplies after him when possible; Franklin accepted this promise but was skeptical that it would be kept (Franklin, 1995).

Progress was slow, even though they were travelling by river. They frequently came across rapids and sometimes they could get away with dismounting the men only and pulling the boat still loaded with supplies across the hazard with ropes, but all too often they were required to unload all the gear, then portage food and equipment followed by the boat to the next safe stretch of river. This happened again and again, eating up days of their time, and one portage would frequently take four or five trips. They were carrying the boat, then returning for the supplies and equipment and having to make several trips because they had brought so much with them (Franklin, 1995). The terrain made travel a brutal proposition; slow, frustrating, full of agonizing miles of heavy hauling. The wilds of North America would not be so generous as to simply open up to Franklin.

Part of the plan that Franklin put together was to hire local Indigenous hunters to keep his crew fed (Brandt, 2010), an acknowledgement that they could not possibly carry enough supplies with them to accomplish their mission. They needed to be able to live off the land at least part of the time. Franklin was taking the advice of Alexander Mackenzie on this point, having sought out the seasoned explorer's advice before leaving England (Brandt, 2010). Hiring local guides and hunters was complicated by the epidemic of whooping cough and measles that was ravaging the Cree and Dene populations through whose territory he needed to travel before arriving at the Inuit Nunangat (Arctic) coast. These diseases had been brought by European explorers just like Franklin, and were so disruptive to the Indigenous populations that even those who weren't sick had begun to starve (Brandt, 2010). As a result, Franklin found it nearly impossible to hire local hunters to keep him supplied. It was a constant issue on this expedition.

Winter arrived and Franklin was forced to halt his movement, taking shelter with smaller HBC forts along the way for the majority of the colder months, not reaching Fort Chipewyan on the shores of Lake Athabasca until 1820 (Franklin, 1995). He had travelled from the western shores of Tasiujarjuaq (Hudson Bay) in what is now Manitoba, across Saskatchewan, and crossed over into Alberta, all either by river or on foot. Fort Chipewyan was an HBC post at the time. Franklin needed to turn north and head for Great Slave Lake where he could pick up the Coppermine River and ride it all the way to the Inuit Nunangat (Arctic) coast. The HBC men at Fort Chipewyan advised Franklin to go to the coast with a crew of at least 20 men for a show of force for the Inuit (Franklin, 1995). The advice he was being given by both HBC employees and the Dene, whose territory he had crossed into, was that the Inuit had a reputation for being warlike, and they shared stories of southern Indigenous peoples being massacred by Inuit men for encroaching on their territory (Brandt, 2010). An element often left out of these accounts, retold by Franklin and others from a eurocentric perspective, is that the Inuit have spent millenia learning how to balance the human population with the food chain in their homeland (Balikci, 1989). A fluctuation of even just a few people can destabilize that balance in a region for decades and put the entire population of the area at risk. This understanding and dedication to sustainability translates into an unflattering portrait from the perspective of European explorers and even Indigenous people from more southern areas. Nevertheless, he managed to hire 16 French voyageurs at Fort Chipewyan to shore up his numbers before turning north and heading for the coast. His party was now closer to 30 people than 20, but it fluctuated occasionally because he had managed to attract some Dene men to guide and hunt for the party, and sometimes the wives of those hunters followed along, although the women had a tendency to come and go as they pleased (Houston & Hochbaum, 2014).

The unwillingness of NWC and HBC outposts to supply his expedition in exchange for chits from the Crown ceased at Fort Chipewyan. He was not only able to double the size of his party by hiring French voyageurs there, he was also given trade goods to offer the Inuit in exchange for food, and three large birchbark canoes (Brandt, 2010). The expedition, now more than a year in, was beginning to look a lot more like what Franklin had planned back in London.

He also had the assistance of a number of Dene people, led by Chief Akaitcho (Brandt, 2010). The beginning of their interactions was rocky, but Akaitcho and his people would be a powerful ally, giving Franklin the benefit of their expertise and hunting local game to help keep the party fed. Franklin was unmoved by these things, and wrote extensively about how fickle and untrustworthy Akaitcho was (Franklin, 1995). But Franklin was not accustomed to negotiating for things, in the navy all he had to do was write a chit and whatever he asked for would be provided; Akaitcho in the beginning was merely trying to get the most out of the arrangement for his people. Franklin also didn't understand the culture or the reasons for the Dene way of life being what it was. It is difficult to live in the northern territories of North America, and the Dene were simply adhering to a way of life that had sustained them in that difficult region for millenia.

Akaitcho would lead Franklin to territory rich with game so they could hunt and build his food stores for the long winter ahead and helped him to understand what to expect from the Inuit when Franklin reached the coast. When Franklin expressed a desire to push for the coast in late summer, signalling his confidence that navigating the coastline on his mapping mission would be a relatively easy and quick task, Akaitcho advised him to build a camp and bunk down for the winter (Brandt, 2010). If they tried for the coast so late in the year they would most certainly die. Franklin was unimpressed, but in the end he took their advice and his men constructed a crude fort of three buildings in which to spend the winter. They were roughly halfway between Great Slave Lake and the Inuit Nunangat (Arctic) coast. They named this crude settlement Fort Enterprise (Franklin, 1995). One of the benefits of this location was they were not yet above the treeline, so there was fuel for fire. There was also a fair amount of game in the area so fresh meat was an available resource. Fort Enterprise was not a comfortable place to spend the winter because Franklin had not brought any carpenters along on his journey. The buildings were crude and drafty, which is a serious flaw for shelter in the region (Houston & Hochbaum, 2014).

During the winter months north of Great Slave Lake, the party was able to kill the occasional fox or caribou that wandered near camp, but they were also forced to eat into their food stores, depleting them when spring came (Brandt, 2010). But winter lingered later than usual that year, and the canoes had become damaged during the winter months. It was necessary to wait for warmer weather so that the canoes could be properly repaired with tree gum, so on June 4th, 1821, Franklin sent John Richardson north to the Coppermine River with 15 voyageurs, two Dene hunters, and most of their supplies while Franklin and the remainder of the party waited to be able to repair the canoes (Franklin, 1995). Richardson and his voyageurs had a miserable trip through deep snow, followed by rain, followed by melt, followed by a great slushy, watery mess north of the treeline. On June 11th they reached Point lake where they decided to stop and wait for the rest of the party, and Richardson sent 13 of the voyageurs back for Franklin and the canoes; without the supplies and scientific equipment, the trip only took 2 days (Brandt, 2010). By mid July, 1821, they had reached the Inuit Nunangat (Arctic) coast via the Coppermine River.

Of the more preposterous elements of this expedition was the use of birchbark canoes in the freezing salt water of the Ukiuqtaqtuup Imavinga (Arctic Ocean). One of the few things that this expedition came close to getting right was the use of small, light watercraft once they finally did get to the ocean, but birchbark canoes held together with tree gum are not optimized for travel over the rough, freezing, ice-filled waters that Franklin put them into (Brandt, 2010). The voyageurs thought he was crazy using them in this way. Incredibly, none of the canoes broke up while travelling in the seawater; such an eventuality would surely have resulted in the deaths of anybody on board. The canoes did, however, all break down from various misfortunes during the next stages of overland travel, ending any delusions they may have had about travelling overwater along the coast back to Tasiujarjuaq (Hudson Bay). The only way out would be to walk.

Before reaching the ocean, Franklin sent ahead 2 translators he had brought along to communicate with the Inuit. Their instructions were to locate any groups nearby and let them know the party was on its way, and they were bringing trade goods to barter for food and supplies. The translators, named Agustus and Junius, encountered some Inuit people, but inadvertently scared them off. For the rest of the expedition, the party would come across the remains of temporary Inuit camps that had been hastily abandoned (Brandt, 2010). The Indigenous population seemed to always know when Franklin was coming, and to do everything in their power to avoid him.

When they reached the sea on July 18th, Akaitcho and his group left. Heading south back to their traditional lands. Franklin also dismissed four of the voyageurs and a handful of other people, cutting his party size to exactly 20. They were at the ocean now, and the expedition could properly begin. Their first day on the water they travelled nearly 50 km east (Franklin, 1996). It must have been an astounding feeling after spending nearly two years travelling overland, perhaps making 12 km on a good day. Franklin was back in his element, leading vessels on salt water.

This first leg of sea travel saw rapid progress, but it would not last long. Being on canoes had the unfortunate consequence of the party being quite low in the water, and it was often difficult to tell if a landmass they were seeing was an island, the coast, or a peninsula. On a ship in clear weather they could look ahead from atop the mast and tell much earlier if they were entering a sound or an inlet, whereas in a canoe it was necessary to probe features more closely to determine their shape (Brandt, 2010). They were on a mapping mission, after all.

Due to this complication, Franklin lost valuable weeks chasing down dead ends, beginning with Bathurst Inlet, which brought them many miles to the south before bottoming out and turning north again. When they finally reached the previous latitude of the coast and began travelling east once more, their desired direction, they were disappointed to find they were blocked, the land masses to their north and south were connected and had finally closed in front of them. They would name this place Melville Sound. Having reached the end of Melville Sound, the party was forced to backtrack to the west again. The closed end of Melville Sound would be the further east Franklin would get on the Inuit Nunangat (Arctic) coast on this expedition. Bad weather trapped them on the shore for a few days, but Franklin led a small party of officers ahead on foot to see if they could see where the land turned to the east again, and they were successful. He called that spot Point Turnagain (Franklin, 1995).

When the weather improved, Franklin was forced to accept that it was time to begin the long journey home. On August 22nd, 1821, the party loaded into their canoes and paddled hard back toward Bathurst Inlet. With a plan to enter the Hood River on the western coast of the inlet, travel to Point Lake, cross overland to the Coppermine River, and continue south to Fort Enterprise. One major complication was that the party was down to its final bag of pemmican on August 22nd, and it could only sustain the party for 3 days on normal rations. This late in the season the caribou begin migrating south, back to the treeline where they are better sheltered in the cold months. Franklin and his party were far enough north that there is no firewood to be had, natural shelter is scarce, and all the game animals the party could hunt were rapidly retreating to the treeline. They were about to be trapped in a very difficult situation (Brandt, 2010).

Franklin decreased the food rations to stretch the pemmican as far as possible, distributing only a small amount each day. They reached the Hood River on August 24th, but Franklin opted to pause there for a few days to give the party some time to rest, and also to break down their canoes and rebuild them smaller so they were better optimized for river travel (Brandt, 2010). They killed three muskoxen during this period and ate well, but when it was time to travel again they were forced to leave most of the meat behind because there wasn't capacity for much additional weight on the smaller canoes. By September 5th they were out of pemmican and fresh meat, and had only a small quantity of portable soup and arrowroot left from their original stores.

On September 7th one of their two canoes was rendered useless when a man fell over carrying it. They used it that afternoon to fuel their fire and cooked the last of their arrowroot and portable soup (Brandt, 2010). That evening they were able to hunt a few partridges, and boiled them in a broth of tripe de roche. This would be their new food staple, composed of a lichen that grows on the surface of rocks. When boiled it apparently has a neutral flavour and is fairly benign. When consumed raw, however, the lichen contains enzymes that help it to digest the rock surfaces where it lives, and those enzymes can cause significant intestinal distress for humans (Potter, 2019). For Franklin and his party, they ate tripe de roche frequently but had limited access to materials to build a fire to properly cook the lichen. Franklin (1995) noted in his journal significant digestive complaints from his party. They would also eat mosses when available, but they were less common than lichen, and when boiled into a broth it was extremely bitter and unpleasant (Franklin, 1995).

The snow began in September, coating the ground and making travel over the rocky terrain very hazardous. Rolled ankles and tripping falls were commonplace. On September 21st, after having abandoned some of their scientific instruments earlier, the party also abandoned the plant specimens they had been collecting for scientific analysis (Brandt, 2010). It was becoming more urgent for them to lighten their load and give them the best chance of making it safely to the treeline before the weather got too cold.

Around this time their last canoe was damaged beyond repair when the man carrying it fell down (Brandt, 2010). The party could no longer take advantage of any bodies of water laid out in the right direction, and traversing rivers and lakes was far more complicated and dangerous without some sort of reliable watercraft. Some men accused the voyageur responsible of destroying the canoe on purpose, a claim which he denied (Houston & Hochbaum, 2014).

They were beginning to starve. Each man had several pairs of rawhide moccasins made by the Dene for them. They began eating any scraps of leather they could find on their uniforms including their worn out rawhide moccasins, thus originating the lifelong nickname that Franklin would endure: "The man who ate his boots" (Brandt, 2010).

A few days after September 25th they came to the Coppermine River and needed to cross it, with Fort Enterprise being just 65 km away on the other side. The trouble was, the water temperature was freezing and the river was over 100 meters wide. Franklin offered a reward to any man who could build a raft from a nearby stand of reeds and get a line across the river (Brandt, 2010). Two tried, but the rafts were only buoyant enough to support one person at a time, they could not build a pole long enough to reach the bottom of the river, and they had only one oar. To make matters worse, there was a strong headwind coming from the other side of the river and it kept pushing the raft back to them. The naturalist, Richardson, attempted to swim across with a line tied to his waist (Brandt, 2010). The idea being that if they could tie the line off on the other side, a man on the raft could pull himself across. When nearly across, Richardson disappeared under the water and had to be pulled back. They wrapped him up in blankets and did their best to warm him up, but "it took hours before he could speak again" (Brandt, 2010, pp. 131). They stripped all his wet clothes off before wrapping him up in a blanket, and the party was taken aback by how skeletal he had become (Franklin, 1995). It was true of all of them, they were starving and burning far more calories per day than they were consuming.

In the days that followed it snowed heavily and the wind continued to be against them. One party member found the antlers and backbone of a caribou, and the party cracked them open and ate the rancid marrow raw. One of the translators that had been employed to communicate with the Inuit, Junius, walked off alone and was never seen again; he is presumed to be the first of the party to die (Brandt, 2010).

On October 4th one of the party members finished constructing a canoe-like craft out of reeds and successfully pulled a line across the river. The rest of the party was able to follow soon after. Once across, Franklin sent a small party, led by George Back, ahead to the south in search of Akaitcho and the Dene; his hope was that they could send supplies. The rest of the party continued south for the shelter of Fort Enterprise. It was troublesome to keep the party together, two men were so weak as to lag kilometers behind the main group. They were the next two deaths on the expedition (Brandt, 2010). Franklin appreciated at this point that his plan was unrealistic, much of the party was too sick to continue to Fort Enterprise, so he split the party in two. He put one of his officers, Hood, in charge of a sick camp; they would bunk down in the first spot with enough trees to provide some shelter and enough fuel for a fire. Richardson and Hepburn also opted to stay, though they were healthy enough to continue, to help care for the sick and try to hunt. Franklin would lead the second party to Fort Enterprise with anyone healthy enough to continue. He was expecting Fort Enterprise to be stocked with food and supplies by the trading companies and Akaitcho based on agreements he had made with them earlier. If he could just reach the fort, he could return to the sick camp with supplies to save his badly weakened men.

Four members of Franklin's party had to turn around and join the sick camp over the next few days. By the time he reached Fort Enterprise on October 11th, he was down to just 5 men (Franklin, 1995). Earlier that year, the plan he had agreed to with Akaitcho was that the Dene would hunt and stock Fort Enterprise with supplies for when he returned from the coast, anticipating that he would have run low at that time. Additionally, he was expecting the thousands of pounds of supplies he had been forced to abandon at the start of the expedition to have been forwarded by the HBC men, as per his earlier agreements with them. But when they arrived at the fort, they found it empty, without so much as a note from either the traders or Akaitcho. Back had been there first, found the fort empty, and left a letter for Franklin explaining that he would continue ahead to find the Dene or perhaps go as far as Fort Providence for supplies (Brandt, 2010). It likely felt like a death sentence. This fort was the light at the end of the tunnel for Franklin and his men, there was to be food and shelter, and the more urgent of those needs was food. But there was none.

The men at Fort Enterprise became weak very quickly, often lacking the energy to venture outside to find *tripe de roche*, and hunting was completely out of the question. Sometimes when they did have the energy, the weather was too cold or windy and they were forced to stay inside anyway. Many days they ate rotten caribou hides that had been discarded at the camp that spring, and pounded bones into dust to eat. The caribou skins were infested with the larva of a fly that is parasitic to caribou; these were especially prized because they were high in protein (Brandt, 2010).

On October 21st Franklin sent the 2 healthiest men at the fort South to look for Indigenous people and ask for aid. He tried going with them himself but was too weak and forced to turn back, there were now just four including Franklin at Fort Enterprise. Too weak to go out and search for firewood, they began ripping planks out of the floor to burn to keep warm (Franklin, 1995). On October 29th, Richardson and Hepburn reached Fort Enterprise to see why food and supplies hadn't yet reached the sick camp Houston & Hochbaum, 2014). They found the four men at Fort Enterprise in a sorry state; only one was well enough to get up and gather firewood. The other three, including Franklin, were too weak to stir from bed. Richardson (1851) wrote that he was shocked by how gaunt they looked, and thought they must have had a similar reaction to his own appearance as well. He had intended to get supplies from Fort Enterprise and bring them back to Hood's camp, but there was nothing to take; moreover he and Hepburn were too weak to go back. They were forced to remain with Franklin and his small group and share in their fate.

On November 7th, three of Akaitcho's hunters arrived with dried meat and fat. Franklin and the men at Fort Enterprise were saved. 11 party members died in total. The hunters nursed the survivors back to health, feeding them, cleaning their bodies and living spaces, and helping them walk south to Akaitchos camp when the men were strong enough to move again (Franklin, 1995). They eventually moved to the HBC facility on Moose Deer Island on Great Slave Lake and spent the rest of the winter recovering from their ordeal.

Along with rescue came letters and information. Franklin was informed that he had been promoted to the rank of Captain, and also that the NWC and HBC had merged and were now both simply HBC; their vicious feud was over. The party also received fresh clothing, having worn the same next-to-skin linens for 3 months (Brandt, 2010).

Richardson documented the events that took place at the sick camp with Hood, who did not survive. Among the four men who left Franklin's party to return to the sick camp in early October was an Iroquois man named Michael Teroahaute; the other three men did not make it to the sick camp, only Teroahaute. Richardson (1851) recorded that Teroahaute was very aggressive with the other men of the party, and argued a lot with Hood in particular. Then on October 18th when Hood and Teroahaute were alone together at the camp there was a gunshot, and Teroahaute called Richardson and Hepburn to come quickly. They found Hood dead, shot in the head, with the Iroquois man standing nearby with his rifle. He claimed Hood shot himself accidentally while cleaning his weapon, and Richardson and Hepburn chose not to challenge him on it. They feared for their own safety because he was still holding a loaded rifle, but they were also certain that he had murdered Hood because the man was shot in the back of the head with a rifle, not the front (Richardson, 1851).

The next day Richardson, Hepburn, and Teroahaute left together for Fort Enterprise. Richardson and Hepburn were concerned because Teroahaute was still behaving in a hostile manner, and felt their only course was to kill him. The two of them had a moment to put a plan together when Teroahaute stopped to gather some tripe de roche, and Richardson decided it was his duty as the ranking officer to pull the trigger. When Teroahaute came back, Richardson shot him once in the head (Richardson, 1851). We have, of course, only Richardson's version of events, so it is necessary to take it with a grain of salt. It does create an interesting distinction for the expedition, however: of the 11 men who died two of them were likely killed by other party members.

It also came to light eventually why Fort Enterprise had not been stocked with supplies by Akaitcho's hunters. When Akaitcho left the party at the mouth of the Coppermine River, he told Franklin that if they continued with the equipment and supplies they had he would assume they were all dead. This in and of itself lowered the priority he placed on stocking Fort Enterprise, but the main barrier was a lack of ammunition. Fort Providence was supposed to provide Akaitcho with ammunition to use for hunting but did not have any to spare. To make matters worse, three of his family members drowned when their canoe overturned in a lake, and in a state of mourning Akaitcho and his people could barely be motivated to hunt for themselves, let alone Franklin (Franklin, 1995). As is often the story, conditions in the north are difficult, and misfortunes tend to compound one another.

The party reached York Factory on the 14th of July, 1822. It was aboard the Prince of Wales supply ship that they sailed for London sometime in early September, reaching home by October. Their long nightmare in the Inuit Nunangat was finally over, though not all of them made it home. Looking to capitalize on a wave of public enthusiasm, the Admiralty pressed Franklin to begin preparations immediately for another overland journey to commence in the spring of 1823 (Brandt, 2010). Franklin had learned his lesson, however. He agreed to return, but not immediately. Any subsequent attempt, he stipulated, would be thoroughly planned out with a long lead time. He would make no assumptions, take nothing for granted, and he understood that any logistical details that were not pre-arranged before he left London were not to be counted on. In the Inuit Nunangat, one must show the appropriate respect for nature. Failing to plan is a deadly mistake.

1825 - Second Land Expedition

When Franklin returned from his first land expedition in 1822, Franklin was a national hero. He gained immediate celebrity status, with dinner invitations flowing in and at some points he was barely able to walk down the street without being mobbed by the adoring public. It was a type of fame he found a little perverse. Franklin seems to have been too introverted to enjoy such attention, being a very charming man but preferring to socialize in small groups. Being the center of attention in a crowd wherever he went was too overwhelming. He wrote to his fiancee, Eleanor Porden of his preference for a select group of friends, and how uncomfortable it was to attend parties and large dinner engagements where strangers all felt the need to lavish compliments on him. Compliments about his adventure seemed to make him feel most uncomfortable. Brandt (2010) notes that in his letters to Ms. Porden, Franklin lamented that people were complimenting him on his success when he felt he had nothing to do with it; it was divine providence that was responsible for his having survived. In truth, it was the Dene who had rescued him from death's door, but he was a particularly pious man and such a dramatic last-minute rescue could not be credited to any mortal being.

Eleanor Porden was a formidable woman, having been spared the typical education endured by women in the 19th century. Her father took her with him in his travels as an architect, inspiring a love of science and literature at an early age. She was a prolific author, and one of her poems, *The Arctic Expeditions,* is what drew Franklin to her in the first place. The two were opposites in many ways, with her writing being witty and vibrant, and Franklin's being wooden and procedural. She loved parties and crowds, he preferred a smaller social circle. They had many disagreements, at one point Franklin suggested that after they married she should stop writing; she refused, and told him if he insisted she would call off their engagement. When he asked her to move her Sunday literary group to another time so they could observe prayer more fully, she refused and he was again forced to back down (Brandt, 2010). Franklin chose for himself a partner that contradicted many of his views, and they certainly did not share the same comfort zone.

Franklin and Porden were married on 6 August, 1823. At that point she had already developed a bad cough. She gave birth to their only child on 3 June, 1824, they named her Eleanor Isabella Franklin. He was deep in his preparations for his next expedition by that time, and Eleanor's health was beginning to fail. Her cough was worse, she was often short of breath, and had trouble climbing stairs (Brandt, 2010). Franklin felt a strong sense of marital duty, and wrestled with whether to cancel his plans to go on his second expedition which was scheduled to leave in mid February, 1825. Finally he made up his mind, he would stay home and support his wife. The preparations had kept him from her far too much, constantly visiting the docks, the Admiralty, and suppliers. He would stop with these preparations and spend time with his family. When he gave her the news, Eleanor wouldn't hear of it. She knew what it meant for him, and that it would almost certainly end his career if he backed out at such a late stage. Once again Franklin had decided on a course of action only for his wife to put her foot down and insist he reverse himself. She had forced his hand, and Franklin sailed as planned. Elanor died just five days later, but the news wouldn't catch up with him for several months.

For nearly two years before he sailed, Franklin was busy making plans for his second attempt. He was planning to be much better organized, and much smarter about his trip. He arranged for the HBC to build facilities for him, had huge amounts of pemmican prepared beforehand, he wanted there to be food ahead of him and behind him at all times. He had learned that living off the land is difficult even for the Indigenous population, and his solution was to ensure there was already food provided. They would still hunt and fish, to varying degrees of success, but he would not count on those activities to provide a sustainable supply of calories (Brandt, 2010). The HBC agreed to their part, and Franklin was well into putting together the other elements of the journey.

John Richardson agreed to lead a second expedition that would travel alongside Franklin until they reached the northern coast, at which point they would separate and explore in different directions. Richardson would explore to the east, Franklin to the west. The HBC built and stocked a fort for Franklin on the shores of Great Bear Lake, which would allow the two expeditions easy access to the Kuukpak (Mackenzie River), which they would use to travel to the sea (Franklin, 1983).

He also knew that he did not want to travel the coastline in birchbark canoes. This time, Franklin had wooden boats built to his specifications, specifically designed for river and coastal travel. They were heavier than the birch canoes, but sturdier as well. He had these sent ahead so they would be waiting for him at the fort. He also constructed a collapsible boat to bring along, one that could be easily stowed and transported but assembled quickly when needed. This sort of item would have made the difference between life and death for many of the men on his first expedition after their last canoe was destroyed (Brandt, 2010).

In early August 1825 they had reached Great Bear Lake and found their fort nearly completed. Franklin intended to call the place Fort Reliance but the HBC had named it Fort Franklin, in his honour. They made such quick time on the journey north, that Franklin actually had time to continue down the Kuukpak (Mackenzie River) to the coast on a reconnaissance mission. The party made it all the way to the mouth of the river and found the sea completely free of ice (Franklin, 1983). It must have been an inspiring sight, precisely what any explorer in the region would hope to see. The ice would not impede their activities if they were to put in and start the journey now. They could not, of course. It was too late in the season. The only prudent choice was to ascend the river and return to Fort Franklin where there was food and shelter to sustain them through the winter.

In June 1826 they returned to the Kuukpak (Mackenzie River) and began their journey to the coast. On the 3rd of July they reached a delta where the river split, and so did the two expeditions. Richardson headed East and Franklin west, they called the place Point Separation. Franklin noted the stark difference between the state of their supplies upon having reached the coast on this expedition in comparison to his previous venture. Food was plentiful and their boats were strong (Franklin, 1983), it must have given him a feeling of great confidence.

On the 7th of July they encountered the Inuit, a group he estimated to number into the hundreds, at the mouth of the Kuukpak (Mackenzie River) on an island. He had brought trade goods along specifically to trade with local populations, but he had not expected to encounter so many. When they approached, the Inuit noticed the large number of trade goods stowed in the boats and attempted to take them by force. Franklin maintained control of his people despite being overwhelmed, many goods were grabbed out of the boats before they could paddle away from shore. The encounter ended when the party fired their weapons into the air and scared off the Inuit (Franklin, 1983). A remarkable element of all these expeditions is just how valuable wood and metal are to many of the Inuit subgroups. Approaching them in heavy boats or even large ships made of wood, filled with trade goods of metal or even surplus food supplies would have been an incredible display of wealth. The concept of ownership held by European explorers was not necessarily shared by Indigenous populations in North America, and many Inuit populations in the 19th century had not interacted with Europeans at this point. It is clear that in the Inuit Nunangat there could certainly be scenarios where explorers could be overwhelmed and interpret Inuit actions as dishonest or even criminal by European standards. Franklin (1983) was certainly clear about his negative feelings toward the Indigenous populations in his journal.

The next day they sailed west along the coast unencumbered by ice, and the day after that on the 9th of July they made more progress before encountering ice that was fused to the shore and extended a great distance out to sea. They climbed the banks to get a better look around and could see no open water or leads to exploit and were left with no option but to wait for the ice to break up or recede (Franklin, 1983). The wind was their friend and enemy. When it blew north the ice was pushed away from shore and the party could advance. When it reversed and blew south they were forced to make landfall and wait. Adding to their frustrations, during the summer months the ground along the coast is extremely swampy and they would sink into it with every step. This made progress by land impossible; there was no option but to wait for the wind to shift in their favour. The nature of their progress was halting. Some days were productive and serious distance was made, on others they could not move at all.

They continued in this manner all the way to Prudhoe Bay by the 18th of August when it became clear the ice would not cooperate and there was no hope of carrying on further. Franklin made a prudent decision to turn around and return to Fort Franklin. They ascended the Kuukpak (Mackenzie River) and were safely at the fort by the 21st of September, 1826 (Franklin, 1983). They spent the winter in relative comfort and departed Fort Franklin on the 20th of February, 1827. Franklin was back home by September that year.

His second expedition had been a remarkable success by comparison to the previous attempt. Nobody had died and they had mapped hundreds of kilometers of the coastline to the west, so while he hadn't rounded the shoulder of Alaska as he had hoped, it was difficult to argue that it wasn't a successful voyage. Unfortunately for Franklin, public enthusiasm for this enterprise of searching for the Passage had waned, and there would not be many exploration assignments coming from the Admiralty. He was now one of their most high profile captains, though, so the Admiralty did go to great lengths to keep Franklin busy.

1827-1845 Life Between the Expeditions

After returning from his second expedition, Franklin began his courtship with Jane Griffin. Another formidable woman, Griffin was stubborn, worldly, and had travelled extensively. She possessed a sharp wit, and was a prolific writer (Woodward, 1951). Jane Griffin possessed many similar qualities to Franklin's first wife, possibly indicating a type. The pair were married on the 5th of November, 1828 (Brandt, 2010), a little more than a year after his return from the second expedition. As demonstrated by the marital drama with his first wife, Eleanor, navy wives were expected to put up with long absences from their husbands. One imagines this could have been a psychologically taxing existence for your typical 19th century English housewife, but Jane Franklin was no ordinary woman. She did not live a quiet existence centered around her husband, she was a prolific world traveller.

When Franklin was given command of *HMS Rainbow*, the 26-gun frigate posted to the eastern Mediterranean sea in 1830, it was a blessing for Franklin's career in addition to his pocket book. He was to patrol the waters near Greece, which had recently escaped the grasp of the Ottoman Empire to achieve independence. The Royal Navy had a vested interest in making sure the proceedings went smoothly (Brandt, 2010). And for Lady Jane it was a great excuse to travel. In 1831 she visited Gibraltar, Morocco, finally stopping in Malta to visit her husband. Quarantine rules were in place, so they could not have any physical contact, but they could stand at a distance and converse; this was made difficult by Franklin's partial deafness from the Battle of Trafalgar (Brandt, 2010). Lady Franklin toured all over Europe while her husband was in command of *HMS Rainbow*, rarely returning home. In fact, when his command was over and he returned home in late 1833, his wife continued to travel for a time. She would not arrive back in England until mid 1834, 9 months after her husband (Woodward, 1951). Brandt (2010) speculates that she had been captured by a wanderlust, having tasted true freedom for the first time and found herself seduced by it. It is a reasonable sentiment, being a woman in such a repressive society and discovering that she had the wealth and ability to go as she pleased must have been fantastically liberating. And for his part, her husband is not recorded anywhere as having been cross about her long absence after she returned home. Any doubt about her devotion to her husband is thoroughly squashed by the lengths she went to in searching for Franklin after his disappearance. She constantly leaned on the Admiralty to do more in the search in the late 1840's and early 1850's, and nearly bankrupted herself by financing so many private expeditions in the decade after his disappearance.

In 1837, after a few years without an assignment, he was offered the post of Lieutenant Governor of Van Diemen's Land (now the island of Tasmania), which he quickly accepted. At the time the empire had stopped all prisoner transfers to Australia, leaving Tasmania as its only remaining prison colony. This complicated life for Franklin because there was no room for maneuver on the prisoners sent to him, they were his problem and that was that. Additionally, there were people on his staff that were fiercely loyal to the previous Lieutenant Governor, and Franklin found himself unprepared for the decidedly political nature of the role (Fitzpatrick, 1949). He had spent his career in the lockstep of military authority, where orders were given and followed. The life of governing a territory, negotiating with subordinates, carrying out orders from London, all the while subjected to the constant barrage of a hostile press, was a life Franklin had not been prepared for.

Matters became decidedly worse in the early 1840's when a major economic downturn struck the island (Fitzpatrick, 1949). He had no power over the market demand for Tasmanian farm goods, of course, but it did not matter any more back then than it does today. When the economy gets tough, people cast blame on their political leaders.

Lady Franklin came with him, of course, but also took the opportunity to travel around Australia and New Zealand. She spent months at a time exploring, always accompanied by her niece, Sophia Cracroft, and on one occasion by her husband. The couple spent a brief period exploring the Tasmanian wilderness (Brandt, 2010). Their adventures into the countryside were one bright spot in the very challenging life they had found for themselves in Tasmania.

Another bright spot occurred when James Ross spent a winter in Tasmania. He had sailed *HMS Erebus* and *HMS Terror* to Antarctica for an expedition, and was lucky enough to spend his winter not locked in the ice, but in the comfort and luxury offered by the Franklin's. Serving with Ross as Second was Commander Francis Crozier, who fell in love with the Franklins' niece, Sophia Cracroft. This was the beginning of an attempted courtship that would go on for several years and see Crozier propose marriage to Ms. Cracroft multiple times (Fitzpatrick, 1949). Another interesting note relates to the ships Ross and Crozier sailed on their Antarctic voyage, *HMS Erebus* and *HMS Terror*, these would be the same vessels used during Franklin's final expedition, and Crozier would serve in the same role (Brandt, 2010).

In 1842 Franklin was relieved of his post as Lieutenant Governor of Tasmania. His dismissal reflected upon his honour, a dark spot on an otherwise clean record (Fitzpatrick, 1949). He had expected the assignment to be challenging, but to earn for himself prestige and elevate his professional status. Instead, he was recalled in disgrace and had his reputation damaged in the process.

Franklin was no longer a young man, it would not make sense to give him physically demanding assignments. But his embarrassment over what happened in Tasmania created an urgency in him to return to the Inuit Nunangat. Back in command of a proper naval expedition he knew he could command successfully, and repair his bruised reputation. He let the Admiralty know he wanted another expedition if they were putting one together. And when it did happen he lobbied hard, calling in favours from friends and eagerly applying for command of the latest attempt (Brandt, 2010). This was not to be an overland expedition, which he himself admitted would not be physically possible at his age and in his physical condition, but to command a ship at sea was perfectly possible. The stage, therefore, was set for Sir John Franklin to sail once more in search of the Northwest Passage.

Chapter 3
Captain Francis Crozier

Introduction

A notable character in the lost Franklin Expedition is Captain Francis Rawdon Moira Crozier, Expedition Second and Captain of *HMS Terror*. One of the few details that is known about the events of the expedition after they lost contact with the outside world is that Franklin died on the 11th of June, 1847 (Brandt, 2010). From that day forth, Captain Crozier was in command of the overall expedition and the most dire decisions likely took place under his authority. For this reason, this chapter will be a brief overview of Crozier and what is known about his state of mind as the expedition was beginning.

Career

Crozier was born in Ireland in 1792, the 11th of 13 children, and joined the Royal Navy at the age of 13 (Brandt, 2010). His first service was aboard *HMS Hamadryad* in 1810. In 1814 while serving aboard *HMS Briton*, he visited Pitcairn Island and met the last surviving mutineers from *HMS Bounty*. He does not appear to have seen any combat in his career, but was able to retain his position and get assignments after the Royal Navy contracted following the Napoleonic Wars. He was an experienced polar veteran, with service in both the north and south. His first expedition to the Inuit Nunangat was with Parry's second expedition in 1821, serving as Midshipman on *HMS Fury*. His second expedition was with Parry in 1824 aboard *HMS Helca*. This was the expedition where, in 1825 *HMS Fury* was damaged by the ice and abandoned. Crozier was promoted to Lieutenant in 1826 and joined Parry's attempt for the north pole over the ice near Spitsbergen (Smith, 2014).

In 1831 Crozier joined the crew of *HMS Stag* off the coast of Portugal during that country's civil war, known as the Liberal Wars. In 1835 he served under James Ross as second in command aboard *HMS Cove* during the search for a dozen lost British whaling ships in the Inuit Nunangat. During his service with Parry, Crozier became a close friend of the younger Ross, and after being promoted to Commander in 1837 joined Ross for a four year expedition to the Antarctic as Second, and Captain of *HMS Terror* in 1839 (Smith, 2014).

During this Antarctic expedition Ross and Crozier stayed with the Franklins in Tasmania. In 1841 Crozier was promoted to Captain. Also during this time period Crozier met Franklin's niece, Sophia Cracroft, and fell in love with her. He would make his first proposal of marriage during this trip. Upon their return to England in 1843 Crozier was elected a Fellow of the Royal Society for his accomplishments in the study of the Earth's magnetic field. His expedition with Ross was an unequivocal success, making a number of important geographical discoveries and penetrating the Antarctic ice further than any previous expedition (Smith, 2014). The success of the Antarctic expedition also served to credit *HMS Erebus* and *HMS Terror* as being well-suited to polar service, and weighed heavily in the decision to use them for the Franklin Expedition (Brandt, 2010).

Final Letter

The final port of call for the Franklin Expedition before their disappearance was at the Whalefish Islands near Disko Bay, Kalaallit Nunaat (Greenland). The crews of the two ships knew this would be their last chance to send mail home until either their successful completion of the Passage or, if they were unsuccessful, their return to the Atlantic side of North America. Among the many correspondences that left the expedition in July of 1845 was a letter from Crozier to James Ross, which contains some interesting details about his state of mind at the outset of the expedition. His letter reads as very affectionate, signalling what in the contemporary vernacular would be referred to as a "bromance" between the two explorers. It must have been a dispiriting sensation for Crozier to be commanding the same ship on this expedition, *HMS Terror*, serving as second officer with *HMS Erebus* in the lead position, but with a commanding officer he didn't trust leading him. Crozier related to Ross how he lacked trust in Franklin's decision making, and believed they were getting underway too late in the season (Crozier, 1845).

Crozier also told Ross about the isolation he felt as Captain of Terror on Franklin's expedition. Typically the second officer of an expedition was given the task of selecting the junior officers, but for reasons that are not entirely clear the Admiralty gave that task to the third officer on the expedition and second in command aboard *HMS Erebus*, Commander James Fitzjames. This decision would have been a clear insult to Crozier, and it also left him with a leadership team aboard his own ship that he did not choose, and he complained to Ross about not having a friend among them. Crozier wrote, "All goes on smoothly but James dear I am sadly alone, not a soul have I in either ship that I can go and talk to." (Crozier, 1845). The tone of Crozier's letter is dreary, but doubly so when compared to the communications of other expedition members at this point. Crewmen relayed feelings of confidence that the Passage would be completed by the following summer. Fitzjames sent home his most recent journal along with a note that told family and friends to expect his next letter from Hawaii in the summer of 1846 (Brandt, 2010). These feelings are understandable and common at the start of an undertaking such as this. While the rest of the crew were in high spirits and excited for the adventure ahead, Crozier lamented the absence of his friends and even remarked on his disappointment at not feeling more enthusiastic.

Other topics discussed in the letter include a new variant of compass provided that he felt was undependable in rough seas, and a number of crewmen he was forced to discharge at Disko Bay due to illness. He also comes out as being totally unimpressed with the locomotive steam engine that had been installed on his vessel, writing, "I will take care it shall not be a steam run - how I do wish the Engine was again on the Dove line and the Engineer sitting in the top of it. He is dead and alive wretch full of difficulties" (Crozier, 1845). It is a fair criticism. Steam technology was still fairly new in marine applications, and there was already a distinction between marine engines and terrestrial locomotives. The engines outfitted aboard *HMS Erebus* and *HMS Terror* were purchased from a rail company and retrofitted to the ships, and could only produce a maximum speed of 3 knots (Brandt, 2010). To make matters worse, each ship was only furnished with enough coal to run their boilers for a few weeks, meaning what little the locomotives could add to their propulsion had to be used exceedingly sparingly. Under such circumstances, Crozier's sentiment can be understood. The locomotive mounted in the heart of his ship was taking up valuable space that could have been dedicated to additional supplies, and worse it had a dedicated staff that was a further drain on his resources.

Crozier's final letter gives a valuable insight into the feelings of the man who was forced to take command of the expedition following the death of Franklin. It paints a picture of an officer unhappy with his position, and lacking enthusiasm for the mission. It also gives us an interesting insight into the personnel, logistical, and technological issues he was managing before the formal start of the expedition.

Chapter 4
Erebus and Terror

A major factor in the events of the Franklin Expedition are the ships *HMS Erebus* and *HMS Terror*, so it is prudent to review the history of the vessels and the technological adaptations made to them in preparation for service in the Inuit Nunangat. While the doctrine of travel held by the Royal Navy was poorly matched to movement through the Canadian archipelago, significant effort and creativity were applied to making the vessels stronger, more comfortable, and more efficient; the specialization of *Erebus* and *Terror* may strike the modern observer as a symptom of the technological renaissance being experienced in Victorian era England. It was a nation populated by people immensely proud of their collective accomplishments, many of which were tied directly to a recent wave of technological competence. This could account for the impression that the Northwest Passage could be navigated if only traditional naval methods were married with updated technologies; public perception was that success in this endeavour was only limited by the creativity of their engineers.

They were partially correct to feel as though they could engineer their way through the Passage, unfortunately the technical expertise necessary was a few generations ahead and the region itself would not cooperate. As Alt (1985) concludes, the Victorian era presented the most unfavourable climate conditions seen in the Inuit Nunangat for such an endeavor seen in the last 700 years. With much of the passage clogged by multi-year ice, the ideal way to navigate the passage would have been to go under it aboard a nuclear submarine, which of course would not be invented for more than a century. But the Royal Navy had a mission to complete and only the technology of their day was available to them, so *Erebus* and *Terror* would be overhauled and made ready for the task.

Much of the information about these two vessels is identical. Both were Royal Navy bomb vessels, conceived of during the Napoleonic Wars (Brandt, 2010). Bomb vessels accommodated enormous mortars on their decks that were to be fired directly upwards to lob ammunition upon enemy vessels and land-based encampments; it was advantageous to strike at an enemy from above because vessels and forts were primarily armoured on their sides, so a well-placed mortar round could devastate the target. This approach produced massive strain on the structure of the vessel, however, necessitating very solid construction. When the wars ended, bomb vessels were thought to be an ideal choice for service in the hunt for the Northwest Passage (Brandt, 2010). Their superior strength would be an asset in navigating waters populated with ice that could crush an ordinary vessel like an egg under a brick.

HMS Erebus was completed in 1826, an order that had been placed during the war with Napoleon but not completed until long after his final defeat. The name *Erebus* derives from Greek mythology, and is a reference to the personification of darkness, and also a region of the Greek underworld where the dead travel through immediately after dying (Online Etymology Dictionary, n.d.). This was a typically dramatic name for a bomb vessel, evidently the Admiralty understood the value of branding when dropping bombs on the heads of their enemies.

Construction of *HMS Terror* was completed in 1813, and saw combat in several battles during the War of 1812. Being of an older design, *Terror* was the smaller of the two vessels. The first polar service of *Terror* was under George Back in his failed expedition of 1836-1837. The ship was nearly destroyed several times, including being forced 12 meters up the face of a cliff, and severely damaged by an iceberg. In total, Back's expedition spent 10 months trapped in the ice and when it was finally freed in 1837, it was taking on water. Back managed a minor miracle in sailing *Terror* home, but time had run out near the end of the Atlantic crossing, they had taken on too much water and the ship was certainly going to be lost. Back made a snap decision and beached *Terror* on the coast of Ireland (Brandt, 2010). This decision allowed *Terror* to be recovered and refitted for future service, which was a mammoth undertaking in itself. It would have been easy for the Admiralty to simply scrap the vessel. The failure of Back's expedition, while disappointing, was seen as a confirmation of the suitability of bomb vessels for polar service. A lesser ship would surely have been destroyed, but *Terror* not only survived, it successfully made the Atlantic crossing in its hobbled condition.

Erebus was sent on its first polar assignment with James Ross on his Antarctic expedition in 1839, accompanied by *Terror* under the command of Commander Francis Crozier (Brandt, 2010). Ross's success in the Antarctic was seen as additional confirmation that these two vessels were well-suited to challenge the ice. They achieved consistent success, crossing the Ross sea twice and Weddell Sea once. Among the important discoveries were the Ross Ice Shelf, and Mount Erebus and Mount Terror (Brandt, 2010). Evidently, the element of luck was not considered when awarding points for success in polar operations.

In preparation for the Franklin Expedition, both ships were given iron plating covering the full profile of their bows, along their sides at the waterline, and wrapping around the stern. Additional thickness was added to their hulls, and their deck planking was cross-laid to better absorb shock. Additional bracing was also added within the vessel to improve hull integrity against the crushing pressure of pack ice (Brandt, 2010). Additional improvements were made, including a desalinator system that allowed them to convert sea water into drinking water, and a crude form of central heating that took advantage of excess heat from the stove to warm water that was run through a series of pipes all over the ship (Brandt, 2010). The heating system was pioneered by Parry in the 1820's and had been adapted and improved in the decades since. One consistent problem with the system was humidity inside the ship and condensation forming on the pipes. The condensation would drip on the crew, and this was particularly irritating in their hammocks because it meant a crewmember at the end of a long day would climb into bed and find it soaking wet. This was mitigated by Parry by wrapping the heating pipes with thick layers of cloth on his expeditions (Brandt, 2010) but it is not clear whether Franklin chose to employ this solution on his ships. In the absence of this heating system, interior spaces on the ships could not be kept warm in the dead of winter. With the outside temperature hovering around -50 degrees celsius, inside spaces filled with warm bodies could often only warm up to -30 degrees (Brandt, 2010).

Both vessels were outfitted with steam engines purchased from the London and Greenwich Railway. The steam engines were used to power a retractable screw propeller mounted aft, making *Erebus* and *Terror* the first two steam powered, screw-propelled Royal Navy vessels. The engines were rated for 25 horsepower each, which enabled a maximum speed of 4 knots (Brandt, 2010). Underwhelming performance, to be sure, but the ability to choose the direction of travel regardless of wind conditions was novel and added options to the toolkit of a captain.

Due to concern that the screw could be damaged by the ice, the propellers were installed with the ability to be retracted up into the ship on demand. An impressive engineering detail that doubtlessly added time to the installation process. It was also recognized that having moving parts beneath the waterline could foreseeably necessitate repairs under water, so the expedition was also furnished with a diving suit. This was also a first for the Royal Navy (Brandt, 2010). It is an unpleasant thought, to be immersed in freezing waters wearing a heavy diving suit with nothing but wool garments to keep warm. It is impossible to know if the diving suit was used during the expedition, but if it was one has to wonder what the total effective time under the surface would have been for the crewmate assigned the task.

Recognizing that boredom was a potent enemy on these expeditions, both ships were furnished with resources to keep the crew occupied during the long idle months of winter. *Terror* had a library containing 1200 books, and *Erebus* was similarly furnished. Both vessels also had school supplies so that illiterate crew members, of which there were many, could be taught to read and write during their down time (Brandt, 2010). *Erebus* was also furnished with a mechanical music device programmed with 50 songs, 10 of which were hymns at the request of Franklin and his deep religious sensibilities (Woodman, 2015). Finally, both vessels were also given a healthy supply of costumes and set-building materials in case they felt inclined to produce a play (Brandt, 2010). It was not uncommon for such activities to be held on this sort of expedition, with the officers performing for the rest of the crew.

The technological exertion and consideration for the entertainment and education of the crew were not novel concepts for Royal Navy expeditions into the polar regions, but for crewmembers who were joining the exploration service for the first time it was likely an unfamiliar element. Lieutenant John Irving (1845) wrote to his sister-in-law in the weeks before their departure that, "Everything has been done that the latest improvements in the various branches of arts relating to nautical matters could suggest; and every reservation against the climate provided for the health and comfort of the crews." While Lieutenant Irving (1845) laments what promised to be a minimum of two years absence on this expedition, he expresses great confidence in the ships, the mission, and the experience of his superior officers, and seemed impressed by the amount of effort dedicated to the comfort and entertainment of the crew.

HMS Erebus and *HMS Terror* were ships purpose built for a war that had ended by the time they were completed. Their uniquely strong design made them a desirable choice for polar service, a theory that was tested many times by ice and weather. With the addition of central heating, libraries, school supplies, and costumes, they were well stocked to keep boredom at bay during long winters locked in the ice. And their technical advancements including steam driven screw propulsion, desalination, and diving suit contributed to their prestige and foreshadowed technologies that would become the backbone of 20th century navies all over the world. Finally, their structural enhancements helped to make them more resistant to the sort of rough service that is required of ships travelling through the Inuit Nunangat, with officers at the Admiralty entertaining big dreams of these ships pushing their way through the ice in the same manner as modern ice-breakers. These were the most advanced ships of their day in any setting, but Franklin and the Admiralty believed they had also employed the cumulative lessons learned in the previous two decades of attempts to navigate the Northwest Passage and made them highly specialized to that purpose.

Chapter 5
Netsilik Inuit

Introduction

In discussing the Franklin Expedition and the methods and technology at their disposal while trapped in the ice, it is prudent to offer the proper attention to the people who have thrived in the region for millenia. Inuit is a term for a broad range of people stretching from the western tip of Alaska to the eastern shores of Kalaallit Nunaat (Greenland), and there exist many subcultures within that vast territory. The subgroup I will discuss in this book is almost exclusively the Netsilik Inuit, who are the people who live in the region where Franklin's ships were frozen into the ice. While many articles and books on the Franklin Expedition do not give adequate attention to the Netsilik, they do get one detail right: the Inuit Nunangat is one of the most difficult environments on Earth for people to survive in. What is fascinating, however, is the knowledge that there are multiple societies that have sustained themselves for longer than any European power has existed.

To describe the Netsilik in the most simplistic possible terms, the thing to know is that the land, sea, and ice of their territory has a massive impact on their lifestyle. To survive, every element of their society has been highly adapted to their environment. The social organization of their communities, migratory traditions, diet, technology, clothing, and spirituality are all highly specialized to survival in their part of the Inuit Nunangat. Their survival is the result of generations of mettle, observation, grit, and determination. A willingness to do what is necessary to survive. Netsilik traditions are extremely focused on the sustainability of the food chain, and are sensitive to the movements of animals through their territory in different seasons. The traditional Netsilik lifestyle is nomadic, and moves from land, to coast, out on the sea ice, and back again as food sources shift and replenish. It is also noteworthy that there are subgroups of the Netsilik based on the specific territory they occupy. Some of these groups rely more heavily on fish reserves, the families from the far eastern boundary of Netsilik territory rely more heavily on caribou for sustenance (Balikci, 1989). In the Inuit Nunangat, the biggest key to life is adaptability.

The purpose of this chapter is to give the reader a reasonable understanding of how the Netsilik traditionally survive. Clothing, diet, hunting techniques, travel, and the overarching doctrine of all these factors will be visited. This knowledge is important in understanding why Franklin's expedition was trapped in such a hopeless situation. It provides the appropriate context for how travel over long distances is possible in the Inuit Nunangat, so that it can be contrasted with how the expedition was equipped and how the officers moved. Eventually the Royal Navy learned to adapt.

It is an unfortunate truth that, despite extensive exposure to many Inuit groups, the Royal Navy did not have the flexibility of thinking to seek out the traditional knowledge of the Inuit. Instead, they sent many expeditions into the Inuit Nunangat, resulting in the deaths of many Royal Navy sailors, but also upsetting the careful balance of the Inuit peoples across the region.

Technology

Technological solutions to environmental challenges are an essential part of life in the Inuit Nunangat. Survival depends on being able to sustain oneself with the materials available to them either in the environment or through trade. While trade did play a role in the traditional Netsilik lifestyle, heavy emphasis is placed on knowing how to get by with only the materials at hand. Most of the Inuit Nunangat is limited in the raw materials generally used around the world for survival, and the Netsilik are remarkably resourceful at using the materials readily available to them. Balikci (1989) describes Netsilik material culture as being divided into four major technological complexes which will be discussed in this section. These are: the *snow complex*, which includes snow and ice. The *skin complex*, covering the use of sealskin and caribou fur, and less frequently musk-ox fur and polar bear skin. The *bone complex*, which encompasses the use of antler and bone but also the rare materials of driftwood and iron. And the *stone complex*, which is primarily focused on the use of soapstone.

The primary character of all four complexes is utilitarianism (Balikci, 1989). Very rarely is an item used that cannot be replaced. The general idea being that a Netsilik individual should be able to either sustain themself indefinitely, or travel to a more suitable location under their own steam.

Snow Complex

The primary function of the *snow complex* is in architecture. The Netsilik are nomadic and in the winter months instead of hauling inefficient shelter with them wherever they go, have discovered that snow is not only readily available wherever they go but is an excellent insulating material. Igloos are made with snow blocks cut with a *pana*, or snow knife, and make great shelter. Snow blocks are also useful for furniture, and windbreaks for sealers and fishermen during stormy weather (Balikci, 1989).

Ice plays a huge role in Netsilik life as well. While it is not a good insulator like snow, during the autumn months the snow may not be deep enough to construct an igloo but the weather is often too cold to live comfortably in a sealskin tent. In this case, rectangular ice shelters with hide roofs are made by cutting and stacking thin river ice. Ice is also useful in autumn to make fish caches in areas where appropriate stones are not available (Balikci, 1989).

Knowledge of the condition of snow and ice is very important, and impacts decisions about where to hunt or set up camp. For example, seals are an important food source but are not found under the pack ice, they maintain breathing holes only through fresh, smooth ice. Not all snow can be used to construct igloos; proper conditions are necessary for snow that can form blocks that can be cut and stacked reliably. This is why there are so many different words for snow and ice in Inuktitut, it is very important to be able to describe the exact nature and condition of these materials (Balikci, 1989).

Skin Complex

This complex is used in the creation of clothing, sleds, kayaks, tents, tools, and thread/thongs for knot tying. The Netsilik have a specific preferred use for each different animal hide and even different parts of those hides for even more specialized applications. The most common materials used in the *skin complex* are caribou hide and seal skin (Balikci, 1989). The materials and preferred uses for them, it should be noted, are not absolute. If the ideal material is not available it is often necessary to improvise with the material on hand.

Caribou hide has thick fur but it is still remarkably light and soft. Each hair is hollow, making it excellent at insulating the wearer against extreme cold. Preparing undergarments and next-to-skin clothing from caribou fur demands an intensive process of curing, softening, scraping, and stretching in various stages. This process provides a comfortable, soft skin that is durable and still warm. For outerwear and sleeping bags, a simpler process is used which leaves the items with a more coarse finish that would not be as comfortable against the skin, but these items also have a greater resistance to snow and are more easily dried when wet (Balikci, 1989). There are different uses for different types of caribou skin as well. The hides of young caribou are ideal for children's clothing. Caribou killed in late autumn have thick, warm hides ideal for bedding materials. Early autumn hides make the best clothing for adults. The hide from the legs of the animal is short haired and very resistant to wear so it is the preferred material for boots and mitts. Caribou hides are even useful once the material has become too worn out for the original purpose. The skin can be cut into long strips, or thongs, used in the construction of kayaks, drying racks, to lace up boots, or any number of other applications. Dilapidated skins can also be stretched and used for drums (Balikci, 1989).

Caribou sinew is excellent material for thread and cord. It is very carefully removed when a caribou is killed to avoid damaging the material. As thread it is used in the creation of clothing, boots, tents, and kayak covers. Simple overcast stitch is used for fur clothing, a blind stitch passing only halfway through the skin makes waterproof seams, and a running stitch is how soles are attached to boots. Sinew is also braided into cords of various thicknesses for bow strings, running strings in clothing, and fishing lines (Balikci, 1989).

Seal skins are the next most useful material after caribou skin, and its uses are equally as specialized. Seal skin is stronger and more durable than caribou, and it is also quite water resistant which makes it especially useful during the warmer, wetter months of the year. The skins of adult female seals are the preferred material for kayaks, scraped and warmed and scraped again to remove all traces of fur and fat to ensure the lowest possible weight for the kayak. The unshaved skins of young seals are ideal for coats and trousers. The curing process is fairly simple and consists of removing the fleshy membrane from the inside surface, washing with snow and water, then stretching and drying by pegging the skin to the ground with enough space underneath to allow air to circulate; the final step involves softening the skins by working them with blunt scrapers before sewing. Seal skin used for waterproof summer boots requires very careful removal of all the hair. A person does this by stretching the skin over their bare thigh and meticulously scraping off every fiber with an Ulu, which is a knife with a small bone or wood handle and a broad curved blade usually carried by females. When all the hair is removed from the outside, the skin is turned over and the process is repeated to remove the blubber. The next step involves stretching and drying the skin in the snow. This curing process produces waterproof but very tough hides, and the material requires extensive chewing to soften it before it can be sewn. Boot soles and heavy duty thongs are made from the skin of great bearded seals because the skin of that animal is particularly thick and durable. Seal skins are also used to make tents, vessels for carrying liquids, packs carried by dogs, dog shoes, sled runners and many more (Balikci, 1989).

Bear and musk ox skins are generally too heavy for clothing items, but can be substituted if there is no caribou or seal available. Bear fur does not absorb moisture, so it can be used fur side down as a sledge if need be. This water-repellant quality also makes bear skin a good material for polishing and icing sledge runners. The most common use for both bear and musk ox is bedding material (Balikci, 1989). Other skins are used as well, though not as commonly. Salmon trout skin makes the ideal container for a tool kit. White fox, wolf, wolverine and dog skins can be used to make trousers, and do a decent job of repelling frost. These also make prized material for hood trimmings (Balikci, 1989).

Bone Complex

Prior to the wide availability of trade goods, iron was not a readily available material in Netsilik territory and therefore not used. Wood is also a very rare naturally occurring material, because trees do not grow at high latitudes; the only wood available to the Netsilik was driftwood, making it a prized and uncommon building material. Bone is the material used in place of wood or metal because it is far more commonly available.

The uses of various bones is as advanced as the different uses for skins, and can be broken down into three important characteristics: size, hardness, and elasticity. The basic material of the bone complex is caribou antler. This is because caribou are such common game animals for the Netsilik, but also the antlers come in reasonably large pieces, are fairly strong, and can be shaped and molded fairly easily. Bear bone is the hardest, and musk ox horn is extremely elastic (Balikci, 1989).

Bone components play a role in the creation of all sorts of tools and implements, the major ones being the bow drill, adze, whittling knife, splitting knife, ulu, saw, antler straightener, drying rack, and kayak frame. Large items require several pieces of antler or bone to be either lashed or glued together. It is common for wood components to be glued together since the pieces are often fairly small. Thongs are used to lash pieces together most of the time, but it is also common to glue pieces together by taking dried blood, moistening it in the mouth, and applying it to the desired surface. The bond from blood glue is so strong that it often does not require any additional support (Balikci, 1989).

Many different components require holes to be drilled, or for the material to be thinned by rubbing against a flat rock, or bent using specially shaped antler implements. Many bone applications require the combination of bone with stone, flint, hide or other materials to complete an item. The bone complex is extremely advanced and complex in its development. Later, as trade with outsiders became more common, metal and wood materials were introduced into the mix and became part of the bone complex (Balikci, 1989). This was one positive development because iron tools last longer than those made of bone and flint, however the Netsilik maintain their ability to create tools from these natural materials regardless.

Stone Complex

The *stone complex* is the final of the four complexes, and mostly covers the use of soapstone for lamps and pots. Soapstone is the most commonly used stone material because it is durable in these uses, but it is also easy to work with. Soapstone is traditionally mined from a location to the southwest of Kuugaarjuk, which is easily reached by sledge in the winter months (Balikci, 1989).

Soapstone lamps are wide and flat bottomed, with a shallow indentation on the topside to hold the fuel, typically some sort of blubber, and wick, often made from dried moss (Balikci, 1989). A single soapstone lamp could be used to keep an igloo warm for an entire family, including melting snow or cooking soup in a pot. They are also used at various stages of drying and curing hides in various skin complex processes. In the summer months, soapstone lamps are not used, which creates seasonal pressure on this resource (Balikci, 1989).

The other primary use for soapstone is the creation of cooking pots. These are made by taking a single block of soapstone and hollowing out the middle by drilling numerous small holes and carving out the middle with a knife, generally the adze. There are also holes drilled through the walls of the pot near the top for suspension cords to be threaded through. Most soapstone cooking pots are between 30 and 61 cm long (Balikci, 1989). The use of cooking pots remains in all seasons, so while soapstone is not needed for lamps in summer the pressure to access this material remains for pots in all seasons.

Subsistence Activities and Nomadic Patterns

Netsilik subsistence activities require a nomadic lifestyle, with winters spent living on the ice and the warmer months on land, with life divided seasonally between activities on the coast and further inland (Balikci, 1989). Difficulty in accessing adequate food resources is the primary driver in Netsilik nomadic patterns, with each season offering opportunities to hunt different game. Most of the primary game have annual migration patterns that present opportunities for profitable hunts, such as caribou and salmon trout. Seals are another primary food source for the Netsilik, and while seals don't migrate, the Netsilik do not have a traditional method for hunting them on open water; as a result, seals are only hunted in the winter when the Netsilik settle on the sea ice.

The seasonal rhythms to Netsilik life also affected the nature of social organization. When harvesting salmon trout, cooperation between family units was necessary for the most efficient hunt, but these hunts were relatively small with only two to three extended families settled in one area at a time. And even so, a fishing weir is typically only fished by a single extended family. By contrast, the seal hunts in the winter require a greater number of hunters for peak performance, so the Netsilik settlements on the ice consist of large groups including several extended family groups in one place that also hunt together (Balikci, 1989).

When it is time to take advantage of the salmon trout migrations with spring breakup, they prepare by stowing their heavy winter equipment that could not be easily transported in the absence of snow and ice. Winter clothing, fresh seal oil from the winter hunt, sleds, drying racks, and soapstone lamps were all stowed in caches where they would be safe until they became useful again the following autumn. The caches were located on high cliffs or small offshore islands where it would be difficult for foxes and other predators to access them (Balikci, 1989).

Salmon trout migrate the same streams every year, and the Netsilik use this knowledge to their advantage. Families hunt the same spot on a migration river every year as well, maintaining stone weirs to channel the fish into a central location. The fish are trapped in this central area, allowing hunters to spear them in large numbers (Balikci, 1989). Salmon trout migrations allow for large stores of food to be built up. Excess fish are stored in large caches, with families digging pits down to the permafrost layer of the soil, lining the pit with cleaned and gutted fish, and covering them up with heavy rocks to prevent predators from eating into the stores. In a good season a family would be able to fill about five of these caches, allowing a security net of food if other hunts were unsuccessful. European explorers in the 19th century routinely noted how Inuit people living on the ice did not appear to save food, often consuming their entire kill on the spot (Brandt, 2010). This habit could be the result of the scarcity of resources in the Inuit Nunangat, with the people learning to go sometimes days on end without anything to eat. If the food situation became particularly perilous, however, the Netsilik often had food caches that could be accessed.

Autumn is the preferred time to hunt caribou. Herds spend the winter south of the treeline where there is some shelter from winter storms, but migrate north in the springtime and occupy coastal regions. Upon first arriving, the animals are skinny and are not the preferred game for Netsilik hunters, but in the autumn they have fattened up and are preparing to migrate south for the winter. When grazing in the summer months, the caribou disperse into small groups or even travel as lone individuals, but as the weather turns cold and the migration south begins, they gather in large groups (Balikci, 1989). This is beneficial for the Netsilik because not only are the animals nice and plump, but they are more approachable when in large groups, not frightening as easily. This hunting period is spent largely inland, with the animals being hunted either on land or as they cross lakes. There are two main methods for hunting caribou. The first being a bow hunt, where a Netsilik man will try to sneak up on an animal and hit it with enough arrows to kill it. The second is the more organized activity of hunting from their kayaks (Balikci, 1989). Kayak hunting is far more profitable, usually allowing hunters to take down enough animals and net enough skins to meet the needs of their family for an entire year. There are different methods for hunting caribou from a kayak, but the general idea is to get the animal into the water using some means of frightening it from the shore. Caribou can swim, but they are much slower and essentially defenseless in that condition. Hunters on kayaks can paddle right up to a swimming caribou and stab the animal with their spear, then tow it to shore using a line. Families will harvest the desired materials from the animals as they go, and cache any surplus meat for later consumption.

The caribou herds thin out as they travel south, leaving perhaps just a few stragglers to be hunted. During this period of low food production, families dip into their caches and non-staple animals are hunted. Fox, sea gulls, ducks, and groundhogs are all targeted, often by children, but none of these activities is profitable enough to meet the daily caloric needs of a family. Fox fur is prized in the skin complex for the trimming of hoods on winter parkas (Balikci, 1989).

When the winter arrives it is time for the Netsilik to make their way out onto the ice for the duration of the cold weather. The only reliable source of food in the winter is seal meat, so the Netsilik have adapted their way of life to go where the food is. The start of seal hunting season can also depend on how successful the caribou and fishing seasons went. If a family has caches of meat available, they will subsist on what they have stored until that runs out. In a poor season they need to head out to the ice and begin hunting seals as soon as possible, but if the other hunts were quite successful, a family may not begin their seal hunting season until as late as February (Balikci, 1989).

There is a great deal of consideration that goes into seal hunting. Seals will only occupy areas of fresh sea ice, avoiding the rougher, older ice left over from previous seasons. Seals specifically seek out smooth sea ice to make their breathing holes. A seal will maintain several breathing holes, visiting periodically to scrape away newly formed ice and keep the small air hole at the top open (Balikci, 1989). Typical sea ice is about three meters thick (Brandt, 2010), so a fully formed breathing hole in the sea ice is a long vertical cone with an air bubble at the top and a small hole through the ice surface. Netsilik hunters use these breathing holes to identify the locations of seals, but locating the breathing holes can be a complicated exercise. On bare ice the breathing holes are easy to spot, but the sound of footsteps on the ice surface scares away the seals. To muffle the sound of their movements, hunters need a minimum amount of snow on the surface of the ice. Too much, however, and it is impossible to find the breathing holes. Dogs are used to sniff out holes and hunters probe the snow looking for their target when the dog signals.

When an active hole is found, a hunter uses one of several methods to indicate when a seal has entered the breathing hole, thus signalling them to strike. But as mentioned, a seal will maintain several breathing holes over a wide area, which is why seal hunting is a group activity. The hunters fan out, each watching one hole for hours on end because there is no way to know which hole a seal will stop at (Balikci, 1989). This method of hunting takes extraordinary patience, and many years to master, but it is an essential skill for long-term survival in Netsilik territory. In addition to providing food and the ideal skins for tents, water-resistant clothing, and kayaks, seals also provide the necessary blubber to fuel soapstone lamps in the cold season. Animal fat, particularly seal blubber, is the only reliable fuel source in the region.

Setting up a winter camp is also a complicated exercise. While seals only occupy areas of fresh sea ice, humans need there to be a significant amount of older ice nearby. Fresh sea ice will contain salt crystals, but after two seasons most of the salt works its way out of the ice. So a winter camp must be set up on fresh sea ice to ensure access to seals, but near a large amount of two year or older ice to ensure reliable access to drinking water (Balikci, 1989).

When living on the ice, igloos are the primary form of shelter used by the Netsilik. Not just any snow is suitable for building igloos, adding yet another condition to the proper selection of a winter camp location. An experienced family can set up an adequate snow shelter in a little more than an hour, however the size and functionality of igloos is also highly variable. Extra wings can be added on to accommodate more than one family at once if necessary, or a house guest, or both at the same time. Thick slabs of fresh water ice are used as windows to allow some natural light in and improve environmental awareness. Furniture inside an igloo is also made of snow; seating, sleeping benches, and a kitchen table are all common furniture items inside snow shelters (Balikci, 1989).

As winter ends and the ice begins to break up, Netsilik families break camp and move inland. The large camps break up into smaller groups that travel together and prepare to begin the cycle over again. Sealskin bags of blubber are cached, with heavy rocks set on top to prevent predators from disturbing the materials, and by the next winter the blubber will have melted into oil suitable for lamp fuel in large enough quantities to last the entire cold season. Winter gear is stowed, kayaks and tents retrieved and redressed/repaired, and the move inland to the fishing weirs begins (Balikci, 1989). The migrations of trout and caribou take place in the same locations every year, so the typical Netsilik family visits the same locations as well. The routine is ancient, efficient, and reliable.

While it took a frustratingly long time for European explorers to apply Indigenous survival principles to their travels in the Inuit Nunangat, they eventually did. The earliest serious interest that the various expeditions showed was for geographical knowledge. There was no better resource for geographical knowledge than the local populations, and most explorers did consult with the Inuit they encountered about geography (Woodman, 2015). As detailed in Chapter 1, Parry had an Inuk woman draw him a map that proved very useful in his exploration of the northern shores of Tasiujarjuaq (Hudson Bay) (Brandt, 2010). Woodman (2015) discusses in detail how both John and James Ross asked the local Netsilik hunters for details of the land on the western side of the Boothia Peninsula while frozen in on the Victory between 1829-32; unfortunately for the Ross's, while the Inuit gave an accurate description of the coastline, channel, and King William Island, there was a language barrier and they were unable to understand the nuance being described. It is interesting that while they clearly took Inuit geographical knowledge seriously, they did not think far enough ahead to secure a proper translator for their expedition. They understood enough to get by in conversation, but they should have known they didn't speak it well enough to understand complex information like geographical descriptions.

In another example of Royal Navy expeditions exploring Inuit technology occurred on Parry's 1822 expedition at Iglulik. His Second, Captain Lyon of *HMS Helca* admired how efficient the Inuit dog teams were. Lyon purchased a team of 11 dogs and began to experiment with their capabilities, noting that a team of three dogs could haul a sledge loaded with 45 kg of supplies a mile in six minutes. In another experiment, his lead dog hauled a load of 89 kg a mile in eight minutes. At one point, a team of nine dogs hauled a sledge load of supplies weighing 732 kg from *HMS Helca* to *HMS Fury*, about a mile away, in nine minutes. Another benefit of the dogs was their navigation skills in a variety of weather conditions; he wrote that he would often travel from *Fury* to *Helca* in blinding blizzard conditions, relying entirely on his dogs ability to find their way (Barr, 2009). It is dumbfounding to think that as early as 1822 Lyon had seen the numerous benefits of dog sleds, but that expeditions continued to use man-hauled sledges for the majority of their activities on foot.

Another noteworthy observation relates directly to the lost Franklin Expedition. Woodman (2015) points out that while many of the choices made by the survivors when they abandoned their ships in 1848 were strikingly odd and inefficient, they had made some modifications to their equipment that appears to be inspired by Netsilik sledges. The crew was set up to load supplies into their ships boats, rest those boats on wooden sledges, and then man-haul those sledges across land and ice to a desired location. This was a standard practice on Royal Navy expeditions in the region, and those sledges are famously very heavy with each man pulling an average of more than 90 kg (Brandt, 2010). Woodman (2015) asserts that the sledges found on King William Island appear to have been modified to reduce their weight. This modification would put them in line with the portion of Netsilik doctrine that asserts the group must travel lightly (Balikci, 1989).This does not account for the bizarre and impractical items they reportedly brought along with them for the trek, but those choices will be visited in Chapter 8 when the symptoms and effects of lead poisoning are discussed in greater detail.

One of the most successful explorers of the Netsilik Nunangat in the mid 19th century was John Rae, the scottish surgeon who was contracted by the HBC to map the coast of Boothia (Brandt, 2010). One of the factors that made Rae so successful was his willingness to adopt Inuit techniques while exploring their territory. He learned how to live off the land and travel light, carrying very little equipment and having become competent enough in the relevant hunting skills to support himself, travelling in a small party of just a few men at a time, using dog teams to pull his sledges, and finally he was competent at building snow shelters (Brandt, 2010). These skills were taught to Rae by the Inuit, and he travelled vast distances over multiple expeditions without ever contending with scurvy or starvation. Rae proved that Europeans could adopt Inuit methods of travel and survival while in the Inuit Nunangat and that their goals could be achieved in the process.

Finally, during the massive search effort subsequent to the disappearance of the Franklin Expedition, dog sleds were used extensively by the search parties (Barr, 2009). This is an approach adopted by the Royal Navy mostly related to communications between ships, because speed was the primary factor. Barr (2009) points out that of the numerous sled parties carried out during the search operations, fully 28% of the km covered were by dog team with the remainder going to the man-hauled sledges. The distance he reports the dog teams covering is 11,500 km.

While the stubbornness of Royal Navy practices in cold climates is difficult to understate, clearly it would also be unfair to imply that no lessons were learned from the Inuit way of life during this time period.

Attempts to glean geographical information from the Inuit (Woodman, 2015, Brandt, 2010), the eventual widespread adoption of dog sleds to carry information quickly over long distances (Barr, 2009), the simple act of reducing the load of the man-hauled sledges (Woodman, 2015), and Rae's complete adoption of Inuit methodology during his expeditions (Brandt, 2010) are all examples of European explorers learning from and employing Inuit knowledge to their activities.

Chapter 6

Franklin's Last Expedition

Now the appropriate context is set. We have discussed the hazards, methods, and attempts from the past to build the basis for Royal Navy knowledge and doctrine in the search for the Northwest Passage. We have discussed the modifications and previous applications of the ships *HMS Erebus* and *HMS Terror*. We have touched on the careers and motivations of Captains Franklin and Crozier. And finally, we have had a brief introduction to the Netsilik Inuit to establish the type of lifestyle and mindset required to survive in the region around Kikertak (King William Island). With this base of knowledge we can finally discuss the events of the Franklin Expedition and hopefully garner some understanding of why they became trapped, and what conditions led to the ultimate death of the entire crew. While there were previous expeditions into the Inuit Nunangat prior to the Royal Navy push starting in 1818 that suffered 100% fatality rates, the Royal Navy had not yet had it's nose bloodied in such a way. Many of their expeditions were unproductive, there had been a few close calls, but overall the fatality rate on expeditions in the Inuit Nunangat had proven no more significant than the majority of Royal Navy service. A handful of deaths and severe injuries were fully expected on any sailing endeavour, and the search for the passage was not exceptional in this regard.

The Franklin Expedition receives a great deal of attention for its mystery, but it is precisely the lack of detailed information that makes detailed examination and timelines challenging. This chapter will review many of the known facts about the timeline, but it will be a brief exercise precisely because there is so little that is directly known. The details here will include references to some of the letters written by the crew leading up to their last port of call, the winter spent at Beechey Island, and the brief exploration of Wellington Channel to make a final test of the open polar sea theory. The archeological evidence will be more closely reviewed in the remaining chapters of this book.

The image of the Franklin Expedition as being extremely carefully planned and executed is conflicted upon closer inspection. When looking at the effort put into the technological efforts invested into the vessels, it is easy to entertain this idea. Upon closer inspection, however, it is striking how long it took for the Admiralty to select the leadership of the mission. Franklin was not the first choice for the job, and there were legitimate concerns over his age and suitability for the mission. After all, he possessed precious little experience navigating the ice aboard a ship, with his most recent being back when he was a Lieutenant in 1818. He sat for an interview with the Admiralty to make his case after pulling every string he had access to in order to get his name on the shortlist to lead this latest search for the Passage. When asked if it were a wise decision to send a man of his age and physical condition on such a demanding mission, Franklin reportedly agreed that he would be an unsuitable choice to lead another expedition overland but quipped that to lead a sea-voyage he needed only to be fit enough to walk the deck of his ship (Brandt, 2010). In a letter to his sister shortly after that meeting, he remarked that he had been selected to lead the attempt (Franklin, 1845a). Herein lies an example of his great ability for charm; it is a fair concern that an overweight, 59 year old man whose only experience navigating ice-filled waters aboard a sailing vessel was nearly three decades earlier. The Admiralty was rightly concerned he was not a suitable choice to lead such an expedition. And yet, even while there were other living officers with more experience and in better physical shape, Franklin got the job.

It also bears highlighting that the letter Franklin wrote to his sister informing her of his new command is dated 8 February, 1845, not even 3 full months before the Expedition was set to leave England (Brandt, 2010). Here we get a glimpse at the confidence and level of comfort Franklin had in his ability to command a seaborne expedition. While he was feeling additional motivation to take on such a mission following his embarrassment as the Lieutenant Governor of Tasmania, this is still a striking departure from the man who insisted on taking two full years to plan his second overland expedition to the Inuit Nunangat. More striking, still, is the confidence he expresses in his letters. When writing to his wife (Franklin, 1845b) and to Parry (Franklin, 1845c) he offers no indication whatsoever of doubt about the success of the mission. To ask Franklin, he was quite certain that his next port of call after Disko Bay would be in Hawaii.

This confidence is displayed among the crew in various degrees as well. Lieutenant Irving (1845), the third officer aboard *HMS Terror*, wrote to his sister-in-law of his confidence in their success, despite betraying some uncertainty related to the unknown. He tells her that while two years is an awfully long time to be away, he doesn't believe they should be gone for more than three. He worries about the danger and unpredictability of the ice, while continually invoking his religious sensibilities to comfort her. The letter is interesting in that he seems to be writing it as much to comfort himself as anyone else, which is a very accessible sentiment considering this was to be his first participation in an expedition to the Inuit Nunangat.

Less confident in the mission and its leadership, was Captain Crozier of *HMS Terror*. Crozier was a veteran of the Inuit Nunangat, and had a healthy appreciation for the humble capabilities of sailing vessels in the face of the ice pack. He had learned caution and patience, a disposition evidently not shared by Franklin. In one of his final communications, he sent a letter from Disko Bay to his close friend, Sir James Parry, saying he was concerned it was too late in the season to attempt a crossing of Sannirutiup Imavik (Baffin Bay) (Crozier, 1845). It was going on mid-July when he wrote that letter and they were just then getting final supplies loaded. He tells Ross that Franklin does not appear to share the same sense of caution, and expresses a deep concern for the success of the mission. All this comes, however, from a deep melancholy he appears to have been struggling with. He laments the absence of Ross and how he feels lonely and isolated from the rest of the crew, even going so far as to say he considers himself more of an observer to the proceedings than a participant (Crozier, 1845). One could dismiss Crozier's melancholy and lack of confidence in his commander as the sort of thing that looks prescient only in hindsight, that in the moment it may not have been as clear which argument held merit. It should be noted, however, that of the three senior most officers on the expedition, Franklin, Crozier, and Fitzjames, Crozier had the most experience navigating a ship through polar waters by a long way. His was the most informed opinion and among the last things he said to anybody in the outside world was that Franklin lacked the caution necessary to navigate the ice.

Last Sighting

When they left England in May the expedition numbered 134 total crew. At their final port of call in Kalaallit Nunaat (Greenland), 5 were sent home; they now numbered 129 between both ships. The expedition set out from Disko Bay on 12 July, 1845 to begin their crossing of Sannirutiup Imavic (Baffin Bay) (Brandt, 2010). As discussed earlier in this book, this is a treacherous region, generally packed with ice being carried on southerly currents to warmer waters. Ice conditions here could make or break an expedition from the start, and Franklin was attempting to cross it fairly late in the season, wasting time here could badly hobble his progress for the first season. Indeed, they were briefly blocked by ice and forced to wait for an opening to present itself. They made this wait along with a pair of whaling vessels.

Franklin spoke briefly with Captain Martin of one of the whalers. Martin claimed Franklin to be in high spirits, and that he said they had been provisioned for five years but could make it last seven with rationing if necessary (Brandt, 2010). This is possibly a miscommunication on Martin's part, since Franklin had been provisioned for three years and it was felt they could stretch it to five with rationing. As Brandt (2010) points out, however, a good portion of their supplies would have been used up by the time the need for rationing would have become apparent so five years is likely a stretch. Captain Martin also did not notify the Admiralty about his conversation with Franklin until 1851. It is possible his memory of the conversation was imperfect after so long, or perhaps he badly wanted to hold out hope for the expedition and if he believed they had supplies for seven years it could set his mind at ease.

The whalers were the last English speakers to have any contact with Franklin. When the ice opened up the vessels parted ways, the whalers on their commercial venture, Franklin toward Tallurutiup Imanga (Lancaster Sound). His orders were to enter the Inuit Nunangat by that route, explore a possible path to the north and test the open polar sea theory yet again on the west coast of Tallurutit (Devon Island) if the opportunity presented itself, otherwise the idea was to travel south, possibly through Prince Regent Inlet, to the northern coast of the continent before making their way west through Ugjulik (Queen Maud Gulf) (Brandt, 2010). The orders were open ended, as can be expected for this type of assignment, but many still felt the best chance to find the passage would be in the bottom of Prince Regent Inlet. Perhaps even Franklin considered this his best option in July of 1845 when he left the two whalers and sailed into Tallurutiup Imanga (Lancaster Sound).

Trail of Breadcrumbs

What is known of the whereabouts of the expedition becomes sparse after the last sighting. From Tallurutiup Imanga (Lancaster Sound) they travelled north up Wellington Channel to the west of Tallurutit (Devon Island) as ordered, to test the open polar sea theory. They must have been blocked by ice because they returned to the southwest corner of Tallurutit (Devon Island) and tucked into a safe bay off a place called Beechey Island for the winter of 1845-46 (Woodman, 2015). It is also reasonable to assume they were blocked by ice to the north because at that latitude the polar ice cap becomes a permanent feature, they would have run into a wall of multi-year ice and seen there was no possibility of success there. Cutting his losses, Franklin turned south and put into the safe haven off Beechey Island for their first winter. It would not have been a surprise. As Captain Crozier was so determined to point out, they had arrived in Tallurutiup Imanga (Lancaster Sound) very late in the season, making the passage in 1845 was always unlikely in all minds except perhaps, that of Barrow, who expressed confidence they could navigate the passage in a single season (Brandt, 2010).

On Beechey Island the crew constructed a small garden, storehouse, a blacksmith's shop, and two cairns, one made of stone and the other out of 700 empty tins of preserved food (filled with gravel to prevent them from blowing away) (Brandt, 2010, Woodman, 2015, Beattie & Geiger, 1989). Some have been confused about the purpose of the tower of cans, but it is entirely possible this was merely a project used to keep the men busy during the idle winter months; crews must sometimes go to extreme lengths to come up with something to do.

They also buried three crew members in the permafrost there, John Hartnell, William Braine, and John Torrington, complete with wooden headstones denoting their names and date of death (Beattie & Geiger, 1989). It is fair to point out that after sending home five crew in Kalaallit Nunaat (Greenland) for illness, and burying three more just six to nine months later, the Franklin Expedition had already experienced an unusually high number of casualties (Brandt, 2010). Having a few serious injuries or even deaths was common even on non-polar service in the Royal Navy at the time, but to experience eight within the first year is certainly well above what would be expected. This has triggered speculation about the overall health of the crew, and suggestions that some factor must have been contributing to this illness; one popular theory being that lead poisoning from the canned preserves weakened the crew and wreaked all sorts of havoc (Beattie & Geiger, 1989). There is much to say on this topic, and it will be discussed in more detail in chapter eight.

When the ice cleared up in 1846 Franklin sailed not directly for Prince Regent Inlet, as many had speculated he would, but west around the north coast of Kuuganajuk (Somerset Island) into Peel Sound. It was believed Peel Sound was a closed bay and the land on both sides was part of Kuuganajuk (Somerset Island) but in fact Peel Sound is a strait, and the landmass to the west is Kinngailak (Prince of Wales Island). By attempting to fill in this blank on the map, Franklin had discovered a strait which happened to be open that year and allowed him to travel deep to the south all the way to Kikertak (King William Island). This route through Peel Sound was not previously known to Royal Navy explorers because in all previous expeditions that passed through the area it had been closed with ice. In 1845 and 1846, evidently, it was open, allowing Franklin to sail in, but Peel Sound was again closed by ice by the end of 1846 and would not open for another decade (Woodman, 2015). Franklin and his expedition were securely locked in by the ice, trapped in a place where not only was it extremely difficult for rescue parties to reach, but that based on their experience in the region other explorers universally agreed was an impossible route for him to have taken.

The expedition was locked into the ice a few dozen kilometers to the northwest of Kikertak (King William Island) at the start of winter, 1846. In a note found in a cairn at Victory Point on the northern coast of Kikertak (King William Island). Dated May 28th, 1847, the message gives the exact location of the vessels at that point, and gives details of their route in 1845 before overwintering at Beechey Island. It ends with the cheerful words "All well" and is signed by Lieutenant Gore and Mate Des Voeux (Brandt, 2010). Late May of 1847 they had just spent their second winter in the ice and were in all probability expecting their route to open up and allow their vessels to proceed within a few weeks time. They likely expected to be able to complete the passage by the end of that season, as the continental coastline was within striking distance and the way from there was well mapped, much of it by Franklin himself.

The final detail that comes directly from the expedition is an addendum to the 1847 note, a second message written on the margins of the paper on the 25th of April, 1848. Nearly one year later and this time the note strikes a much more sombre tone. The expedition was beset by ice on the 12th of September, 1846, and the ice had not released their vessels in the summer of 1847 as expected. Running low on food and supplies, the decision was made to abandon the ships on the 22nd of April, 1848. Sir John Franklin, it says, died on the 11th of June, 1847, just two weeks after the first note was written. Furthermore, 9 officers and 15 crew had died in total, a strikingly high number indeed. It claimed the remaining 105 crew were setting out the following day on foot for Konajuk (Great Fish River) (Brandt, 2010), which is located far to the south, across Kikertak (King William Island) and beyond Ilivileq (Adelaide Peninsula). The distance from where they were to where they were going, measured in a straight line, is roughly 330 kilometers. The actual distance travelled would be much farther when considering obstacles and the shape of the coastline the party would have been following.

From this point on, the information about where they ended up and what they did is the result of artifacts, human remains, and Inuit testimony. This information belongs more comfortably in chapters 7 and 8, and will be reviewed in depth. To date, no additional notes or documents of any relevant substance have been found from the expedition; the sparse first-hand testimony from the crew ends, and the search for answers begins.

Chapter 7

The Search for Franklin

After Franklin's departure from England, the only option for everyone else was to wait. The relevant question ultimately became one of how soon is too soon to worry? When should it be treated as an emergency? A few were surprised when Franklin did not emerge in the Pacific by 1846, but there was not yet cause for alarm. Still more found it surprising that the expedition had not turned up by 1847, but again, it was well within the assignment to be gone for that long. To ask the Admiralty, there was not yet cause for alarm. In fact, even on the expedition itself they likely did not see themselves as being in need of rescue as the summer of 1847 faded into winter. Command likely saw their situation as strained, and one way or another they would need to make it to a port somewhere in the summer months of 1848, but there was no need to panic just yet. The unpredictable variable was not their food supplies, they were provisioned for full rations for three years; but nobody could say how fast or how hard scurvy would appear. Many crews on previous expeditions began to show signs of it by the end of the first winter. But this was not always the case. Sir John Ross's crew on *Victory* did not become heavily afflicted with scurvy until after several years.

Sir John Ross told Lady Jane Franklin that if the expedition had not been heard from by February of 1847, he would lead an expedition himself to find them. Refusing retirement at the end of 1846, he wrote a letter to the admiralty in January of 1847 that it was clear Franklin had not reached the Bering Strait and was likely beset by ice near Ilulliq (Melville Island). Ross proposed that an expedition be sent through Tallurutiup Imanga (Lancaster Sound and Barrow Strait) to search for him and deposit supplies on the southern coast of Ilulliq (Melville Island). The Admiralty denied this request, claiming to have consulted other experts on the subject including Barrow, the younger Ross, and Parry, and that rescue was not yet warranted (Brandt, 2010). Franklin was amply supplied and not yet in danger of starving, even if they had not begun rationing their supplies. While this is true, Ross was making a valid point about how to successfully support expeditions to the Inuit Nunangat. If Franklin did come to need supplies, planning and dispatching a resupply or rescue mission in 1848 was too late, it would take at least a year for the rescuers to reach them, and that was assuming they knew where to look.

The change in execution that Ross was proposing is one that was employed and scaled up in the subsequent ten years once concurrent rescue missions were being mounted. Constant communication and resupply, periodic scheduled contact between vessels of different expeditions would increase the safety of operations in the Inuit Nunangat, but at considerable expense. In one case this approach even saved the crew of a vessel that had been beset in the ice near Ikaariaq (Banks Island) some years later while participating in the search for Franklin's lost expedition (Brandt, 2010).

Around the time Ross was writing letters to the Admiralty requesting a ship and crew to mount a rescue mission, the Admiralty was beginning to quietly consider what such an operation would look like. They consulted with the experienced explorers about what could be reasonably done in case Franklin did require aid. On their advice, the Admiralty dispatched a small party of volunteers overland to deposit caches of food and supplies along possible routes they believed Franklin might take, with the party leaving England in June of 1847 and joined the next year by John Richardson and John Rae (Brandt, 2010). The plan was to travel overland along the coast to deposit supplies, search for Franklin and his men, and consult the Inuit for any local knowledge.

Rae, as a matter of fact, had completed an expedition just the year before that began in Repulse Bay near Naujaat and trekked overland to the Boothia Peninsula and back again. Interestingly, this overland journey to the west coast of the Boothia Peninsula put Rae within 200 kilometers of where Franklin and his men were. Despite talking frequently with the local population, Rae was completely unaware of Franklin's presence because Franklin was trapped in an area rarely visited by the Netsilik (Woodman, 2015). The unique element of Rae and his various overland expeditions was his tolerance for and adoption of Inuit methods; he took the time to learn Inuit techniques of hunting, clothing, travel, and shelter. He travelled with a relatively small party, moved by dog sled, carried shockingly few supplies with him by Royal Navy standards, and survived off the land wherever he went (Woodman, 2015). These methods would make him among the most successful and furthest travelled English explorers of the Inuit Nunangat, and he never had a fatality under his command. The purpose of his 1846-47 expedition was to probe the coastline and determine if Boothia was a peninsula, as he believed, or if there was a passable strait separating Boothia from the mainland, as the Admiralty and most of the Inuit Nunangat veterans of the Royal Navy believed. Rae came up just short of answering the question, leaving a small gap on the map where a possible strait could exist. He argued it was definitive enough since there was no indication of tides or currents that would suggest the presence of a strait. Rae also reported that the Netsilik did not have any knowledge of Franklin's expedition. Nor did he expect them to, after all it was generally felt that Franklin's route would have taken him far to the north of that region through Tallurutiup Imanga (Lancaster Sound and Barrow Strait) and in the winter of 1846-47 there was almost nobody ringing the alarm bell. And while Franklin was in reality just a couple of hundred kilometers to the west of Rae's party off the northwest coast of Kikertak (King William Island), the Netsilik were unaware of his presence because the west coast of the island is notoriously short on game (Woodman, 2015). As discussed earlier in this book, Netsilik behaviour is heavily influenced by the migration patterns of their food resources, so there was no reason for them to spend time in an area that was not along the migration routes of caribou or salmon trout (Balikci, 1989).

Dressing Up Foxes

By early 1848 when nothing had been heard, the alarm bells began ringing at last. The Admiralty sent three expeditions that year, including the one led by Richardson and Rae overland. Their mission was to descend the Kuukpak (Mackenzie River) to the coast and search along the coastline to the east, burying supplies and equipment as they went. Franklin's orders were to find the northern coastline of North America, if possible, and follow it west to Bering Strait (Brandt, 2010). It was a fair assessment to send a party to that stretch of coastline. It should be noted that the last time Richardson followed that coastline was in 1826, during his and Franklin's twin overland expeditions. Richardson was Franklin's age; impressively he was still physically fit enough to lead an overland expedition. Something that Franklin had notably admitted he would not have been capable of.

The second two expeditions went by sea. One, under the command of

Thomas Moore aboard *HMS Plover*, was sent west to Bering Strait. They would follow the coastline with small boats exploring as they went, and travel east to Barrow Point, which Franklin had reached in 1826 before being turned back by fog and ice (Brandt, 2010). The third expedition was led by Sir James Ross with *HMS Enterprise* and his second officer, Edward Bird, commanded *HMS Investigator*. His orders were to follow Franklin's course through Talluriup Imanga (Lancaster Sound and Barrow Strait). Ross, it should be noted, was the first man the Admiralty had asked to lead the 1845 expedition, but he turned it down because of a promise he made to his wife some years earlier that he would take no more of these missions to the ice. Franklin's disappearance, evidently, was enough to shake him from retirement and send him back out into the cold. The younger Ross knew those waters better than perhaps any Royal Navy officer alive, and he would have known he had the best hope of finding Franklin (Brandt, 2010).

These first three search expeditions were unsuccessful in turning up any evidence of the Franklin Expedition. The one that carried the greatest hopes for success was that of James Ross, but there was nothing but poor luck in his effort. The ice in Sannirutiup Imavik (Baffin Bay) was backed up and delayed his entrance into Tallurutiup Imanga (Lancaster Sound) until late August. The summer was almost completely over and they hadn't begun the search yet. Prince Regent Inlet was clogged with ice and impassable. Another line in Franklin's orders was to explore Wellington Channel and test the open polar sea theory once more, but Ross found that route solidly blocked by ice as well (Markham, 1909). During this entire effort, Ross stopped periodically to build cairns and bury food caches along the shoreline for Franklin to find if he happened to pass through the area.

Ross put his ships into a place he was familiar with on the north of Kuuganajuk (Somerset Island) called Leopold Bay and they stayed there for the winter. No effort was spared in attempting to think outside the box. The crew was desperate to come up with something productive to do after having such an unsuccessful first season. They began catching wild foxes and outfitting them with copper collars. The collars were engraved with the locations of the ships and the food caches, the hope being that someone from Franklin's crew might catch one and find the information useful (Markham, 1909). Unfortunately, foxes are territorial so the net effect of this effort was that Ross and his crew spent the winter in the company of a group of well-dressed foxes that never left the vicinity of *Investigator* and *Enterprise*.

When spring of 1849 came, Ross sent out four sledge parties to search in different directions. Brandt (2010) notes that this was to become the standard model for all the search expeditions; ships would sail as far as the ice would allow them, find a safe harbour to spend the winter, and send out sledge parties to do a thorough search in the spring. In 1849 for the crews of *Enterprise* and *Investigator*, it was an especially miserable exercise. They had no dogs to help with the hauling, there was not enough food, and most of the parties returned to the ships sick with scurvy after such intense and prolonged work on so few calories. The party led by Ross followed the north coast of Kuuganajuk (Somerset Island). When they reached the point where the coast turns south, they found Peel Sound full of multi-year ice, and they were still under the assumption that it was a sound not a strait. This was the place where it was later discovered Franklin had gone south, but there was no indication for Ross that it might be the case. Another party explored south all the way to Fury Beach and found the remaining supplies there still in excellent condition. Nothing of note was discovered by any of the parties (Markham, 1909).

The summer of 1849 was characterized by unusually stubborn ice. Ross was unable to cut his way out of Leopold Bay until late August, with hopes of exploring Wellington Channel but the pack ice moved east into Tallurutiup Imanga (Barrow Strait) and beset the ships once again. When it released them several weeks later, they had been carried all the way out into Sannirutiup Imavik (Baffin Bay). It was September and scurvy was already becoming prevalent on both ships, so Ross made the decision to return home (Markham, 1909). All three of the first search efforts came up empty handed, not finding so much as a cairn or a stitch of clothing from the Franklin Expedition.

Urgency at Last

Lady Jane Franklin, disappointed by the lack of progress, offered a reward of £3,000 to any ship that came to Franklin's rescue. Her move was smart on multiple fronts, first in giving incentive to the whaling fleet to consider undertaking the mission, and second in embarrassing the government into offering their own reward. Not to be outdone by the wife of one of their captains, parliament voted to offer £10,000 to anyone offering news of the expedition's fate, and £20,000 to anyone who found survivors (Woodward, 1951).

Lady Franklin's efforts to find her husband would continually apply pressure on the government to best her efforts. She had the attention and sympathy of the public, and she had a considerable fortune at her disposal. Between 1850 and 1859, she personally funded five separate expeditions in search of her husband. So fixated was she on the effort that she nearly bankrupted herself; Woodward (1951) notes that her father disowned her in the mid 1850's after failing to convince her to give up the search. It was pointless, he told her, there was no sense spending her entire fortune to hunt down the expedition when the entire crew, including her husband, had certainly died by that time. Her marital duties had been fulfilled, nobody could have expected her to do more. But Lady Franklin pressed on, demonstrating a stubborn determination that is repeatedly demonstrated through the events of her life, but never more so than in the search for her husband.

1850 was the year that true urgency found the search for Franklin and his men. Brandt (2010) writes that it was the largest and most expensive search effort of the 19th century. The Admiralty that year sent two ships from the Pacific side, an additional six Royal Navy vessels from the Atlantic, two American vessels privately donated and staffed by the United States Navy joined in, and finally Sir John Ross privately raised funds after being denied by the navy yet again and set out in a small schooner, towing his own yacht along with him. He had promised to go in search of Franklin and even at 72 years old, he intended to keep his word. Finally, Lady Franklin sent a ship of her own in 1850 with money she financed from friends, but mostly out of her own pocket (Brandt, 2010). There was a fleet headed to the Inuit Nunangat that year in search of Franklin.

In August of 1850 came the first true lead. The ice in Tallurutiup Imanga (Lancaster Sound) pushed the rescue vessels to the mouth of Wellington Channel right past Beechey Island at the southwest coast of Tallurutit (Devon Island). The first to be pushed into the area by ice were the Americans who found a pair of cairns, a ring of stones indicating a tent had been erected at the spot with the stones used to weigh down the sides, and the omnipresent litter that coincided with all European activities in the Inuit Nunangat. They took the cairns apart in search of a note, as was the custom, but found nothing. They left their own notes behind and rebuilt the cairns as they had been found. Wellington Channel appeared to be open, and they opted to seize the moment and chased off north with urgency (Brandt, 2010).

Within days the rest of the fleet had been forced into the same spot by the ice, ten vessels in total anchored off Beechey Island all at the same time. It must have been a frenzy of activity as the crews scoured the island for clues. They found the remnants of a storehouse, a garden, an armourers shop, and a cairn carefully constructed out of some 600 empty food tins, carefully filled with gravel to weigh them down and arranged in a tower. Everywhere they looked the ground was littered with cordage, tarpaulin, wood, clothing, pieces from broken furniture, and more. It was clear that Franklin and his men had spent considerable time in this place (Brandt, 2010). The final piece of evidence at Beechey Island supplied some important details: three graves of crewmen from the two vessels dated January and April, 1846 (Beattie & Geiger, 1989). Although Franklin had not left a note on the island, it was clear from the headstones that he had spent his first winter in this place.

Among the discoveries were sets of sledge tracks heading up the east coast of Wellington Channel, apparently Franklin had sent men to investigate the ice conditions along that avenue in the spring. The tracks were partly notable for how deeply the sled runners cut into the earth. As Woodman (2015) points out, Franklin had evidently not learned the lesson of travelling light in the Inuit Nunangat if his sledges were so heavily laden as to make deep tracks that still appeared fresh after five years.

The discoveries on Beechey Island set off a frenzy of public attention and hope that survivors might be recovered. And while the findings were significant, they also merely provided a starting point. Franklin had not left any indication as to which path he would take next. For years to come, ships and overland expeditions would explore the Inuit Nunangat along what were considered the most likely paths. Sledge parties would search the coastline, vessels would routinely probe into Prince Regent Inlet and stop by Fury Beach to check if Franklin had been there, Kiiliniq (Victoria Island), Ikaariaq (Banks Island) and Ilulliq (Melville Island) were investigated multiple times. Ross the elder released hydrogen balloons to drop colourful pamphlets over the widest possible area with messages of encouragement and the locations of cairns and food caches for Franklin to find. Sledge parties travelled tens of thousands of kilometers every year. Yet despite this sustained effort, no new information was gained about the fate of Franklin or his crew. The net result of these efforts was a rapid expansion of geographic knowledge of the region, and even the first crew to navigate the final stretch of the Northwest Passage by ship via the narrow strait between Kiiliniq (Victoria Island) and Ikaariaq (Banks Island) (Brandt, 2010). These expeditions were not easy. Many sailors lost toes, ears, fingers, and even hands and feet to frostbite. More still died of exposure while participating in sledge parties. But despite the heavy investment of human capital and financial resources, none of these parties found the information they were looking for. None knew what happened to Franklin or the 125 other men with him after they left Beechey Island.

The Netsilik Connection

By 1853 there were a handful of active expeditions still searching for Franklin, but the great push was beginning to wind down. Very few believed that there could still be survivors, and while the public was fascinated by the mystery, the lack of new information caused interest in the Franklin Expedition to wane. John Rae was no longer concerned with the search for Franklin. He had gone on multiple expeditions overland, personally covered tens of thousands of kilometers by dog sled and on foot, and for all his efforts the most he had discovered was a scrap of wood on the coast of Kiiliniq (Victoria Island) that may or may not have belonged to *Erebus* and *Terror* (Rae, 1953). He was the only explorer at the time to adopt Inuit methods of survival and knew what it took to sustain a person in the Inuit Nunangat for long periods of time. Brandt (2010) writes that while many of Rae's contemporaries believed that if the Inuit could survive in the region, Royal Navy men could do it better. Rae suffered from no such hubris. He did not believe such fantasies about the infinite capabilities of Royal Navy personnel, and knew first hand that most other explorers had no idea how to properly exist in such extreme environments. In other words, Rae had given up any hope of finding survivors. There was no reason to believe Franklin's crew could survive for such a long time, they would have succumbed to starvation, or exposure, or scurvy, or some combination thereof. It was an inescapable fact. So solving the mystery of Franklin's disappearance was not anywhere in the pitch Rae made to the HBC when he proposed another expedition to Boothia in 1853. He wanted to finally close the last gap he had left behind on the map in 1846-47; he wanted to return to that place and definitively establish that Boothia was indeed a peninsula.

In the spring of 1854, Rae had made it to Pelly Bay, which is the furthest south end of Prince Regent Inlet and was headed west to the coast of Boothia before he planned to turn north and map the last remaining stretch in the area. He encountered two Netsilik men who agreed to travel with him for a few days and act as guides. In conversing with them, one of the men, named In-nook-poo-zhee-jook told him of a group of 35 or 40 "kabloonas", or white men, who had starved to death to the west of the great river a long distance away (Woodman, 2015). Rae offered to purchase any items the Netsilik men had from the kabloonas, including a gold cap band that was a standard issue for Royal Navy Officers. He did not, however, pursue this lead beyond conversing with the Netsilik. Rae continued north and completed his mapping expedition, a choice that was harshly criticized when he returned to England. Rae justified himself by saying his expedition was being funded by the HBC to map the coast of Boothia, not to go in search of Franklin. At any rate, the kabloonas had been dead for at least four years, according to the Netsilik, and their description could have referred to any river from Konajuk (Great Fish River) to the Kuukpak (Mackenzie River) 1,600 kilometers away. He was not equipped for such an expedition (Rae, 1953). It was a fair point.

On that expedition, Rae filled in the last blank on that part of the map. Kikertak (King William Island) was an Island, and not connected to Boothia by a land bridge, as assumed by James Ross in 1831. Boothia was a peninsula, and there was no strait connecting Pelly Bay to Simpson Strait south of Kikertak (King William Island). His long-delayed work in the area was concluded, the map was filled in (Brandt, 2010). Before leaving the area, however, Rae made time to meet with more Netsilik to ask questions and acquire more artifacts from the kabloonas who had starved. Among the artifacts he purchased was a silver spoon with the initials F.R.M.C. carved into it. The assumption being that they stood for Francis Rawdon Moira Crozier, Captain of *HMS Terror* and Franklin's second in command (Woodman, 2015). Other artifacts included coins, plates, a scalpel, and a bronze star awarded to Franklin by the British government in recognition of his service in Greece commanding *HMS Rainbow* (Brandt, 2010).

In speaking with the Netsilik, Rae was told that none of the people present had been in contact with the kabloonas, but they had spoken with others who had. They relayed a story about encountering a party of men near the south west coast of Kikertak (King William Island) who were dragging sledges, they looked gaunt and malnourished, and their mouths were all hardened and black. The presence of kabloonas in their territory had been unknown to them up to that point, so they were wary of the strangers who seemed to have appeared out of nowhere. The west coast of Kikertak (King William Island) is notoriously short on game and the ice is generally multi-year in Qaggiujaq (M'Clintock Channel), so seal hunting is not done there. They claimed this was the first time any of them had contact with the men from the two ships beset in the ice off

Kikertak (King William Island). None of the men present spoke Inuktitut well enough to be understood, but with hand signals the kabloona leader, who introduced himself as Aglooka, seemed to give the impression that their ships had been crushed. Aglooka and his men were headed south to where they could find some caribou to hunt. The Netsilik gave Aglooka a bag of seal meat and spent some time with the kabloonas. The oral histories are conflicted about whether the Netsilik spent one day camped with the kabloonas on the shore or five, but they did not immediately part ways (Woodman, 2015). What is clear is that Aglooka did not want the Netsilik to leave, and he and his party may have tried to keep up with them as they crossed Simpson Strait to the mainland but were too slow.

The location of the dead kabloonas is called Starvation Cove. The Netsilik told Rae that the bodies found there were mutilated and there were human remains inside the cookware. It was made clear to him that they had observed indications of cannibalism among the final survivors; they had resorted to eating their fallen crewmates. Some of them must have survived a while longer, they told him, because shots had been heard and fresh feathers and goose bones were found nearby on the Adelaide Peninsula (Rae, 1953).

With his mapping mission completed and his newly purchased artifacts, Rae returned home to England. He received broad criticism for not doing more to investigate the claims of his Netsilik hosts, and many in British society accused him of being a fool. Clearly, they argued, the Netsilik were lying. Theories ranged from the Netsilik having overwhelmed and killed the crew themselves and were just trying to cover up their misdeeds, to having probably eaten the crew as well (Brandt, 2010). This racist response was all too typical and Rae did not win any friends with his unhappy news that not only were Franklin and his men dead, but they had resorted to the unthinkable last resort of consuming human flesh at the very end. The return of Franklin's bronze star did, however, once and for all convince Lady Franklin that her husband was dead. She would fund only one more expedition to the Inuit Nunangat, this time not to rescue her husband but to search Kikertak (King William Island) for clues about what happened (Brandt, 2010).

Rae was thoroughly denounced from all sides including the newspapers, the Admiralty, Charles Dickens (who was a personal friend of Lady Franklin), and everyone in between for suggesting that Royal Navy sailors could be reduced to such unspeakable acts. He was not knighted for his discovery, although most other explorers who went after him to

Kikertak (King William Island) were. What he did get out of it was the £10,000 reward offered by parliament for information about the fate of the expedition, which he quietly collected (Brandt, 2010). The information was also apparently good enough to close the case for the Admiralty, because they moved all members of the Franklin Expedition off of their active crew lists and declared them dead (Kaalund, 2020). Rae never returned to the Inuit Nunangat again.

Although convinced of the deaths of the expedition members by the Inuit accounts passed on by Rae, Lady Franklin was disgusted by what she perceived to be a character assault on her husband with the suggestion that cannibalism took place (Brandt, 2010). Rae's account had left many questions unanswered for Lady Franklin, and to his credit he visited her upon his return to offer his condolences. There had been a time just six years earlier when she had called on Rae's mother to endear herself to him, but after his revelations he was likely the last person in the world she wanted to see. One of the most pressing questions on her mind was, the Inuit account relayed by Rae claimed there were only 40 men present, what happened to the rest? She wanted to know if they had broken up into multiple parties and headed in different directions, what had caused them to abandon the ships, and where the ships were (Brandt, 2010). As previously discussed, Lady Franklin had the resources at her disposal to fund private expeditions, so she did just that.

She engaged the explorer Leopold McClintock for one final expedition to the Inuit Nunangat to explore Kikertak (King William Island) and search for answers to these burning questions. Aboard the steamer Fox, McClintock and his small crew departed England in July 1857. The expedition stopped in Kalaallit Nunaat (Greenland) for one last resupply before heading for Tallurutiup Imanga (Lancaster Sound), and purchased a number of trained sled dogs (Kaalund, 2020). McClintock was taking the advice of one of his Inuit guides, and his three sled parties would make extensive use of the dogs to lighten the load and increase their reach. This is a notable detail because while dog sleds were used on prior search expeditions, the previous attempts still favoured man-hauled sledges while dog sleds were used primarily as courier and communication services between ships. McClintock was the second explorer after Rae to make use of dog sleds as his primary mode of travel.

The ice did not cooperate with McClintock, and he only reached Beechey Island in August of 1858. He attempted to travel through Peel Sound as Franklin had done in 1847, but were forced to turn back due to ice and reroute around Kuuganajuk (Somerset Island) and into Prince Regent Inlet. They found Bellot Strait, which separates Kuuganajuk (Somerset Island) from the Boothia Peninsula but is typically frozen from coast to coast with multi-year ice. This year it was open, so they sailed through to see if Peel Sound was open further down. It was not, and the party wintered in an inlet in Bellot Strait for the winter of 1858-59 (Brandt, 2010). It was not a huge roadblock for them, from Bellot Strait they were within striking distance of Kikertak (King William Island), with Victory Point being just 270 kilometers to the south. Sledge parties on previous search expeditions had travelled greater distances in fairly short periods of time, but McClintock's use of dog sleds greatly increased the range and efficiency of his sled parties. In the fall his party made several journeys to the south to set up supply depots for use in the spring, and one group travelled to Fury Beach and reported a sizable stack of soup and vegetable tins still neatly stacked and edible after 36 years.

On April 2nd, 1859, McClintock dispatched three sled parties. One went to examine the coast of Kinngailak (Prince of Wales Island) to their West, another he sent down the west coast of Kikertak (King William Island), and McClintock led the final party down the east coast of Kikertak (King William Island). McClintock began hearing Inuit accounts and buying up relics of the Franklin Expedition at this time. Most of what he heard confirmed what Rae had said, although McClintock would omit the cannibalism angle in his report (Kaalund, 2020), but he also heard accounts of the ships. One oral history talked about a three masted ship crushed by the ice, although all the men got off safely. Another more mixed account relates how one of the abandoned vessels was forced ashore by the ice, the Inuit were forced to cut a hole in the hull to gain access and found a corpse on board. Later as the ice receded, the ship was carried into the water and quickly sank because of the hole in its side. The confusion in this account has to do with the supposed location of this ship, there were multiple sources for the story and McClintock's translator was fluent in the Inuktitut dialect from the eastern regions of the Inuit Nunangat, but not the Netsilik variation from the central region. Geographical descriptions were often too difficult to be understood accurately. McClintock believed this vessel had been forced ashore on the northwest coast of Kikertak (King William Island), but later accounts placed that ship on the coast of the mainland further to the south (Woodman, 2015). The Inuit claimed to have gotten a large portion of their wood and metal resources from the ship forced ashore, and made it clear to McClintock that they had scavenged a large portion of the Franklin Expedition sites in the decade since (Brandt, 2010).

It should be noted here that in the history passed on by Rae, the story of the ship being crushed originally stemmed from Aglooka communicating with the Inuit via hand gestures where he appeared to describe a ship being forced onto its side by the ice and then sinking. While Woodman (2015) discusses some isolated accounts of Inuit having witnessed the crushing of that vessel first-hand, it appears that interpretation is exaggerated. Perhaps the ship was forced onto its side, and there may have been damage, but both *HMS Erebus* and *HMS Terror* have since both been found in 2014 and 2016 respectively, and both vessels are in remarkably good condition. No signs of the dramatic crushing described in some oral traditions. The assumption made by researchers and authors prior to the 2016 discovery of *HMS Terror*, including Woodman, was that the crushed vessel was *Terror* and that it would not be found because it was thoroughly destroyed in deep waters and the debris field would not be covered in a thick layer of silt on the seafloor. The confusion is understandable because reliable translators of Inuktitut were simply not available to the expeditions of the time.

McClintock purchased silver plates bearing the Franklin crest and some relics from other officers on the expedition, and continued south. He made it all the way into Chantrey Inlet onto Montreal Island where they found a few scraps of metal that could only have originated from the Franklin Expedition, but nothing of great importance, so they turned north and returned to Kikertak (King William Island) (Brandt, 2010). It was important for McClintock to visit Montreal Island because an HBC overland expedition from 1855 had reported relics there, but were forced to turn back inland after that point. Montreal Island is just under 100 kilometers from the mouth of Konajuk (Great Fish River), where the Inuit had told Rae and McClintock the survivors were headed (Brandt, 2010). It is conceivable that once they reached Chantrey Inlet, the survivors may have found it open and been able to sail their boats instead of continuing the gruelling exercise of hauling sledges.

Upon his return to Kikertak (King William Island), McClintock located the first human remains from the expedition. On the south shore atop a gravel ridge laid the skeleton of a young man dressed in the weathered scraps of a naval uniform, he appeared to have died on the march and fallen in the position in which the party found him. Nearby were a set of brushes and combs, causing McClintock to speculate the man had been a ship's steward (Brandt, 2010). The position of the body also alluded to something McClintock had been told by the Inuit, that they died as they walked along and most were left as they were (Woodman, 2015).

Continuing to follow the south coast of the island, they came across a number of cairns which they opened but found no notes inside. Eventually he encountered a cairn from his other sledge party that was sent down the west coast of the island, telling of the discovery of the cairn and note at Victory Point on the north end of Kikertak (King William Island). This critical piece of information is to this day the only formal report to have been discovered from the Expedition. The original note was signed by Lieutenant Gore and Mate Des Voeux in May 1847, and relates their location in that year, the attempt to pass through Wellington Channel and winter at Beechey Island, although it contains an error in claiming they spent the winter of 1846-47 at Beechey Island when it was actually the previous winter of 1845-46 (Brandt, 2010, Woodman, 2015, Beattie & Geiger, 1989).

There was an additional note, written around the margins, signed by Captains Crozier and Fitzjames, and dated April of 1848. Notably, Fitzjames, who wrote the margin note (Woodman, 2015), did not notice the error in the original message. This message claims the ice never released the vessels in the summer of 1847, and after being beset by the ice for an additional winter the ships were abandoned. Crozier added that they were setting out for Konajuk (Great Fish River) the following day, although he did not specify whether they intended to find escape there or were looking to take advantage of the annual caribou migration that would soon pass through the area as a desperately needed source of fresh meat (Woodman, 2015). Finally, Fitzjames's note also gives June 11th, 1847, just two weeks after the original note was dated, as the date Sir John Franklin died. There was no cause of death listed.

The most common interpretation of the Victory Point note in combination with Netsilik accounts is that the crew, running low on supplies and heavily affected by scurvy, were marching out to Konajuk (Great Fish River) with the intention of rowing all the way up to Great Slave Lake where they could find rescue with the HBC. They marched in one large party and had all died by the winter of 1848 (Brandt, 2010). Woodman (2015) draws some interesting conclusions that point in a different direction, drawing heavily on the Inuit testimony and how establishing dates for many of the Netsilik interactions with the survivors is not a clear-cut exercise because the Netsilik were often unsure of exactly how many seasons had passed since these interactions. The timeline is confused more by the fact that many of the oral histories were second-hand stories being told to imperfect translators more than ten years after the events took place. While there is an incredible level of detail preserved in the Inuit accounts, the English fixation with dates and numbers is not shared in the traditional Netsilik lifestyle. We will discuss Woodman's theory further in the next chapter, but the broad strokes are that the ships may have probed the eastern side of Kikertak (King William Island) in 1846 after navigating Peel Sound to test the blank spot on the map and the possibility that Kikertak (King William Land, as it was known to them) was actually an island and not connected to the Boothia Peninsula on its eastern side as assumed by James Ross in 1831. The ships would have found it impossible to clear the shoals of Matty Island because their draft was simply too deep, and would have been forced to turn back to the west where they were beset by the pack ice in September 1846. The cairn at Victory Point may have been established as a supply depot to support the sledge parties carrying out scientific readings and exploration on Kikertak (King William Island), and was later used as the primary staging camp when the ships were abandoned. When the march for Konajuk (Great Fish River) began, Woodman (2015) speculates that the crew did not travel as one mass but broke up into multiple parties, including some that were tasked with maintaining caches of food along the coast for the larger parties, with one senior officer leading a large party down the west coast of the island (the featured party in Rae's Inuit testimony), and another party having crossed the island to travel down the east side. He also cites testimony that very small teams may also have remained aboard both ships in case the ice opened up. Finally, Woodman (2015) discusses the possibility that while much of the crew died in 1848, some may have lived as late as 1850.

Following the revelation of the Victory Point note, McClintock continued to follow the south coast of the island and rounded the southwest cape and turned north to travel toward Victory Point. Along the way he came across a site now known as "the boat place" (Woodman, 2015), where a ships boat from the Franklin Expedition sat atop a sledge with two skeletons inside, there were more human remains nearby in what was left of a canvas tent, and a great quantity of clothing, food, and other assorted items. McClintock noted the odd detail that the sledge was pointed north, not toward Konajuk (Great Fish River) but toward Victory Point and the ice-locked ships (Brandt, 2010). He also calculated the weight of the sledge at 635 kg, and that was without the addition of supplies and sick crewmen that can be assumed to have also been carried on the sledges (Brandt, 2010).

At Victory Point, McClintock was struck by the volume of material that had been moved ashore by Franklin's men. Many of the items did not make sense to him, including metal rods, iron rings, a stack of now-rotted clothing four feet high, and a medical kit containing many still-sealed vials of medicine for low-level ailments such as indigestion and sleeplessness (Woodman, 2015). He also noted other items at locations between the boat place and Victory Point including rings of stones indicating European tents had once been set up at those places, with artifacts including heavy cast iron stoves, pick axes, shovels, and old canvas (Brandt, 2010).

McClintock returned to Fox from Victory Point and found his other two sled parties had already returned. They set out right away for home, trying to make it out of the Inuit Nunangat before winter set in because some of the crew were already suffering from scurvy. They made excellent time, arriving in London on September 21, 1859 (Brandt, 2010). Upon his return, with his artifacts, Inuit testimony, and the note from Victory Point, the Royal Navy opted to retroactively fund the expedition. Parliament awarded McClintock and his crew a reward of £5,000. McClintock was knighted for his effort. He was hailed as a hero for his discoveries, and escaped the controversy that dogged Rae, largely because McClintock made no mention of cannibalism in his account (Brandt, 2010, Woodman, 2015).

McClintock's expedition had unlocked the mystery and located what is to this day the most important artifact from the Expedition: the note from Victory Point. The British government would fund no more search expeditions for Franklin Expedition artifacts, and were satisfied with his findings. However, McClinktock's expedition was not the last. An American eccentric, Charles Francis Hall, became obsessed with the Franklin Expedition and believed it was his destiny to find survivors somewhere near Kikertak (King William Island), the Adelaide Peninsula, or the Boothia Peninsula. In 1864 he set out on a personally funded expedition to Kikertak (King William Island) and surrounding areas. Hall discovered more human remains and artifacts, he heard many of the same stories from the Netsilik, but unsurprisingly failed to locate any survivors (Woodman, 2015). He became fascinated with the Inuit Nunangat, however, and met with an unusual end in 1871 during a U.S. Government-funded expedition to reach the geographic north pole aboard the research vessel Polaris. Hall fell suddenly ill after drinking a cup of coffee, and after a few days his condition improved. He accused his shipmates of poisoning him during this period before the return of the symptoms and his resulting death. The doctor on the expedition determined the cause of death to be apoplexy, although an autopsy conducted a hundred years later found arsenic poisoning to be the likely cause of death, and it should be mentioned that one of the men Hall accused of his poisoning before he died was the doctor on board Polaris (Woodman, 2015).

The next notable expedition was funded by the American Geographical Society and led by U.S. Army Lieutenant Frederick Schwatka from 1878-80. The mission was to search for Franklin Expedition papers they believed to still be on Kikertak (King William Island). They did not find papers but they again heard the oral histories from the Netsilik that had been told to Rae, McClintock, and Hall. They also found more relics, and recovered bones who they believed belonged to Lieutenant John Irving of *HMS Terror*. The remains were returned to his native Scotland and buried with full military honours at a church in Edinburgh in 1881 (Brandt, 2010).

Both Hall and Schwatka relied extensively on the Inuit for knowledge and methodology to travel and survive in the Inuit Nunangat, with Schwatka going to similar lengths as Rae to adopt the Indigenous methodology. He travelled with a small party by sled dog, wore traditional clothing, and carried very little food and relied on what game he could kill to feed himself (Woodman, 2015). To some degree or another, every search expedition to visit Kikertak (King William Island) relied on traditional knowledge, and their discoveries would not have been possible without the contributions of the Netsilik.

Chapter 8
Modern Analysis

Fascination with the Franklin Expedition has maintained interest in the general public since the Victorian era, but it was the 1984 autopsy of Petty Officer John Torrington and 1985 autopsies of Able Seaman John Hartnell and Private William Braine on Beechey Island led by Dr. Owen Beattie from the University of Alberta that triggered a renaissance of direct academic study of the tragedy. Following the wealth of information found on Beattie's various expeditions, other researchers have been inspired to conduct their own research, with a wealth of information having been published in the decades since. In this chapter, we will discuss several of the more recent conclusions that have been drawn by researchers, including the case for cannibalism, lead poisoning, zinc deficiency, and the work of Dr. Owen Beattie culminating in the autopsies of the three bodies buried on Beechey Island. An impressive body of research has been formed in recent decades, encouraged further by the discovery of both sunken vessels. They paint a picture of the final days of the expedition, and lend some light to the details of the oral histories provided by the Netsilik people, who bore witness to the events. While our picture has become more complete, we also see that most answers only raise further questions. A direct and detailed account of the expedition will never be known, but as research continues we can attempt to better understand the condition of the crew and the decisions they made.

Beattie Expeditions

Owen Beattie made his first trip to Kikertak (King William Island) in 1981 in search of human remains. He did locate a number of bone fragments, which he collected for later analysis, many of which turned out to be Franklin Expedition members and others were Netsilik remains

(Beattie & Geiger, 1989). Beattie and his team started their investigation by visiting Starvation Cove, the place first reported by the Netsilik to Rae and later visited by Schwatka, but they found their research to be nearly impossible due to the low lying ground being saturated by the summer meltwater. Later that evening the researchers asked their Netsilik hosts about any potential gravesites on the southern coast of Kikertak (King Wiliam Island), and were given some leads to pursue. Near Booth Point they investigated a potential burial site, and one of the researchers discovered skull fragments that the party thoroughly catalogued. The group also located several limb bones which appeared to match the physical characteristics of the skull fragments, leading Beattie to think the bones all belonged to a single individual (Beattie & Geiger, 1989). The location was a former campsite of the Franklin Expedition, marked by the characteristic ring of stones typically found where a tent had at one time been erected. Beattie noted that the bones were all located near the entrance to the tent, and that while they appeared to belong to a single person, there was a striking lack of certain bone fragments such as rips, spinal column, and the three bones that make up the pelvis. This unusual distribution of bones may have been caused by animal activity; the odd distribution was noted and the work continued. All the party found were some skull fragments and limbs. Also apparent on these bones were the characteristic pitting and scaling often associated with scurvy, it left little doubt in the researchers minds that the Franklin Expedition was suffering badly from its effects (Beattie & Geiger, 1989). Other skeletal remains were found during this expedition, but all proved to be those of Inuk individuals who died in the 18th, 19th, and 20th centuries and were unrelated to Beattie's research.

Upon his return to the University of Alberta, Beattie sent samples from the collected bones off for chemical analysis and worked with his colleagues to review field notes from the expedition. The bones and their unusual distribution at the campsite returned some unsettling results. The researchers were able to clearly identify tool marks indicating they had been intentionally processed with tools such as saws and knives. It was not possible to mistake the markings with animal activity because the narrow, straight cut marks were clearly made by metal implements, particularly under a microscope, the shape of the markings was indicative of intentional cuts. There were also fracture marks on the leg bones indicating that the bones had been intentionally broken. Also notable is that of the skull fragments, no facial bones were present. It is common in episodes of survival cannibalism for the victim to be dehumanized, including mutilation of the face, to make the act psychologically easier. This could explain why there were no facial bones present; those bones may have been damaged and discarded as part of the dehumanization of the corpse. This was the first indication by a modern researcher of cannibalistic activity on the Franklin Expedition (Beattie & Geiger, 1989). Beattie (1989) also theorized that cannibalism could explain why only arm, leg, and skull bones had been found. If the corpse had been dismembered for the purpose of consumption, it was likely done at a different location with the missing parts having been consumed there. Arms and legs contain major muscle groups that are easy calories, and they are also more portable than a human torso. The group that made their camp near Booth Point may have carried the dismembered parts of their crewmate with them for later consumption (Beattie & Geiger, 1989).

Upon their return the following year, the team planned to retrace the steps of McClintock and Schwatka, to travel along the west coast of Kikertak (King William Island) and use the notes and journals of the Victorian explorers as a resource to locate additional sites. They hired a twin otter plane to fly them over their planned route from Resolute and up the coast, dropping supplies along the way to reduce the weight the researchers needed to carry with them. They stopped in Gjoa Haven to pick up an additional team member before flying to the northwest tip of the island to begin their expedition. The plane dropped them off five kilometers north of Victory Point and left them to make the long trek down the west coast of the island.

That coastline is very isolated to this day, but during Franklin's time when the Netsilik practiced their traditional nomadic lifestyle, it was not a place commonly visited. The west coast of the island was a famously poor hunting ground, and the ice tended to be multi-year ice unsuitable for the seal hunt (Balikci, 1989; Woodman, 2015). There is game present, and some hunting can be done, but nothing suitable to sustain a group as large as the Franklin Expedition. Migration routes bring caribou across Simpson Strait to the south shore, which disperse inland and across to the east coast. Fish populate several sizable lakes on the island, and many species of fowl are attracted to the fresh water as well. The west coast is home to foxes and the occasional polar bear, but any group of people passing through the area cannot count on living off the land and must rely on the food they carry with them (Woodman, 2015). Unfortunately for the crews of *Erebus* and *Terror*, the west coast of Kikertak (King William Island) would offer little to no fresh meat to help alleviate the scurvy they were likely suffering from.

Beattie's party scoured the camp near Victory Point for relics, but there was little significance remaining at the site. There are clear indications of European activity there, but the dramatic evidence observed by McClintock has long since rotted away or been removed. The party collected a few items and searched for any indication of graves in the area, but were unable to locate human remains. The group soon began their long journey south (Beattie & Geiger, 1989).

The west coast is also notable for challenging terrain. The low-lying coastal areas are transformed into enormous and exhausting mud-flats in the summer months as meltwater runs out into the sea. There are also rivers that run from the inland lakes out into the ocean and pose significant obstacles to people travelling on foot. The loose stones on the ground are characteristically sharp and difficult to walk on, and shred even modern footwear. In many places it makes more sense to venture out onto the ice and hug the coastline as closely as possible, which it is assumed the Franklin Expedition was forced to do; pulling heavy sledges loaded with supplies through the mud would simply not be possible. Beattie's team experienced these difficulties first hand with their heavy packs, and remarked on how physically demanding the activity must have been for Franklin's men, pulling sledges while malnourished and weak from sickness (Beattie & Geiger, 1989). Beattie's 1982 expedition demonstrated the difficulty in traversing the west coast of Kikertak (King William Island). They did locate a few more bone fragments, but overall they were unable to locate the burial locations noted by McClintock or Schwatka, finding that any markers in that vast landscape blend in with the terrain too easily, making it difficult to find remains once they are buried. The most significant finds on the 1982 expedition were made at the Boat Place, where artifacts such as a tobacco pipe, some wooden relics, and some human remains were found, including the bones of a complete human foot. The party also located the sole of a boot with metal tacks pushed through it, evidence of makeshift cleats to improve traction while hauling heavy sledges across ice (Beattie & Geiger, 1989).

When the expedition was completed and Beattie returned home, he found results for the chemical analysis of the bone fragments from his 1981 expedition had arrived. The Netsilik bones contained lead levels within the established norm of 22 to 36 parts per million. Results from the Franklin Expedition crewman, on the other hand, had a reading of 228 parts per million. A level this high would indicate the person was suffering from lead poisoning. This unexpected discovery leads Beattie (1989) to consider possible sources of lead contamination on the Franklin Expedition, and while the list is extensive, most researchers have focused on the lead soldering of the tinned foods as the culprit.

High lead levels were also observed in the bone fragments collected on the 1982 expedition, and provided additional evidence of scurvy. But lead poisoning cannot be diagnosed from skeletal remains alone, and this fact is what brought Beattie to think about seeking permits and funding to conduct the autopsies of the bodies buried in the permafrost on Beechey Island. It was the only place known where there may be some soft tissue preserved from the Franklin Expedition. Beattie assembled a research team and conducted one autopsy on Beechey Island in 1984, and repeated the procedure on the remaining two graves in 1986 (Beattie & Geiger, 1989). The research teams had to use pickaxes to dig down into the permafrost, and at times found themselves questioning whether there were any bodies in the graves at all because they were buried so deep. When they did reach the bodies, they found this depth in the frozen earth ensured the excellent preservation of all three bodies, and thus complete autopsies were possible including the collection of various types of tissue samples for later analysis. All three men yielded extremely high lead levels, and appeared to have lost a great deal of weight in their final months, likely due to illness (Beattie & Geiger, 1989).

Beattie's research team theorized that due to poor diet and extensive lead exposure, these crewmen had significantly suppressed immune systems and likely fell ill with tuberculosis (Beattie & Geiger, 1989). Confirmation of this diagnosis was not possible because in being frozen, significant cellular degradation had occurred which prevented conclusive tests from being conducted. Subsequent research conducted by Forst & Brown (2017) attempted to detect the presence of DNA belonging to *Mycobacterium tuberculosis* in Private William Braine's tissue samples. Their analysis found none of the relevant DNA in samples taken from his ribs, implying that he may not have died of tuberculosis. The absence of those DNA sequences in such extreme conditions, however, does not eliminate the possibility of tuberculosis as the cause of death altogether, it merely does not provide confirmation of Beattie's theory (Forst & Brown, 2017).

Zinc Deficiency

Recent research has also challenged the theory that lead poisoning played a significant role, at least in the death of John Hartnell, who died in January of 1846 and was buried on Beechey Island. Christensen et al (2017) conducted micro-X-ray fluorescence mapping, stable isotopic measurements, and laser ablation inductively coupled plasma mass spectrometry to analyze the lead, zinc, and copper levels of Hartnell's thumbnail and toenail samples. The average growth rate of these tissues is slow enough that by measuring the various levels of these metals across the entire length of the nail, a timeline of these levels can be established spanning several months.

This analysis showed that for John Hartnell, while the lead levels on the exposed portions of his nails saw a high level of exposure, lead contained on the non-exposed layers actually decreased as the expedition carried on, and his internal lead levels were within the normal range for an English person of his era. What was not in the normal range, however, was his zinc. Christensen et al (2017) therefore theorizes that the diet of the crew of the Franklin Expedition did not contain adequate micronutrients. This may have played a role in suppressing his immune system, perhaps playing a role in his ultimate death from tuberculosis and pneumonia or some other respiratory ailment. When the body is zinc deficient, the metabolism of vitamin A is affected, and a lack of both these nutrients has a negative effect on the overall immune response (Christensen et al, 2017).

It is also the case that the tinned foods, procured by the Admiralty from a company called Goldner, had improperly sealed the food tins, leading to a significant number of the containers going rancid and perhaps being contaminated with botulism (Christensen et al, 2017; Brandt, 2010). If the preserved foods had gone bad in significant numbers, Chrsitensen et al (2017) speculates, this could explain why Netsilik accounts from the crew's long march describe them as appearing horribly emaciated. Perhaps they were short on food after all, or perhaps enough food had gone bad that they didn't trust even the tins that appeared to be in serviceable condition. While Christensen et al (2017) acknowledge that this test was conducted on a single individual who died two full years before most of the crew, Hartnell's case could potentially signal an issue of malnutrition with the rest of the crew. This could also help explain why between the end of May, 1847 and the end of April, 1848, the margin note reported that nine officers and 11 crewmen had died (Christensen et al, 2017). Such a high fatality rate could be the result of severe malnutrition among the entire crew.

The Case for Cannibalism

The first talk of cannibalism was reported in England by Rae after he was told by the Netsilik of the site now known as Starvation Cove. The Netsilik repeated these claims whenever their histories were requested by outsiders looking for answers about the Franklin Expedition, although some, like McClintock, chose to downplay or completely omit these accounts (Brandt, 2010). Beattie discovered bones with telltale cut marks and weathered postmortem breakages indicating cannibalism on his 1981 expedition to Starvation Cove and Kikertak (King William Island) (Beattie & Geiger, 1989; Mays & Beattie, 2016). This evidence represents vindication for the Netsilik accounts of the last days of the expedition.

Survival cannibalism progresses in a consistent and generally predictable sequence. First, the large and easily accessible muscle groups are harvested, typically starting with glutes, thighs, calves, and arm muscles (Mays & Beattie, 2016). As the starvation scenario progresses, more effort is put into processing the corpse for food, moving to muscle groups on the torso, followed by the organs, and as the situation becomes more desperate, more effort is put into processing the body. Veins, tendons, and skin are consumed as the surviving party becomes increasingly hungry and is pressured to put aside their psychological reservations, with hands and feet generally processed and consumed around this point as well. Features identifying the body as human are avoided early in the process to aid with the psychological strain of seeing a human corpse as a source of meat, so body parts that are most easily dehumanized are favoured for consumption (Beattie & Geiger, 1989). This may involve the removal of hands and feet, and the covering or mutilation of the face, or sometimes decapitation. Once the face is removed, the brain is generally extracted and consumed through either the opening at the base of the skull or through the facial region, particularly when the face has been mutilated in the early stages. The final stage of survival cannibalism is the processing and consumption of bone marrow. To access the marrow, the bones must be cracked open, taking considerable strength; it is not uncommon for the bones to be boiled to facilitate the extraction of the fats and oils found in the marrow to make a drinkable broth (Beattie & Geiger, 1989; Mays & Beattie, 2016). Outside factors can affect the progression of survival cannibalism and change the order of some consumption, but in a static scenario without outside pressures like travel affecting the outcomes, the sequence of corpse processing is generally the same. One example of outside pressures is observable in the remains recovered on Beattie's 1981 expedition, where calories located in the skull and limb bones were consumed last. In that case, Beattie & Geiger (1989) theorized that portability of the corpse took precedence over the typical progression of the cannibalism scenario.

Organs and torso muscle groups are assumed to have been consumed first in that case because the skull and limbs were easier to transport for use as a food source at a later time.

Beattie's 1981 discovery of cut marks and post-mortem breakages is strong evidence for end-stage survival cannibalism, but Mays and Beattie (2016) conducted research that convincingly establishes that end-stage cannibalism did occur on the Expedition. Post-mortem breakages can indicate the dismemberment of a corpse for cannibalistic purposes, but the placement of those breakages can also indicate that the starving party was attempting to access the bone marrow, which are the most labour intensive calories to access on a corpse. By analysing the bone fractures, researchers can observe the presence of a phenomenon known as "pot polish", where fractured bones are placed in boiling water and the fractured edges form a smooth finish (Mays & Beattie, 2016). The only reason to break and then boil bones is to facilitate the extraction of bone marrow. Mays & Beattie (2016) analyzed 418 skeletal elements from the Franklin Expedition representing a minimum of 17 people, and positively identified cut marks, breakages, and pot polish, on 107 bone fragments representing at least seven individuals. In simple terms, the bones of at least seven crew members of the Franklin Expedition were boiled by other survivors to access the very last calories contained in the corpses. This finding also vindicates the specific Inuit oral histories that claim human remains from the Franklin Expedition were observed in the cooking pots of some locations, including Starvation Cove (Woodman, 2015).

Woodman's Reconstruction

In his reconstruction of events, Woodman draws some interesting conclusions based on the oral histories of the Netsilik, in combination with analysis of the Victory Point document, and orientation of many of the archeological sites. One curious detail that Woodman (2015) discusses was first observed by McClintock when he discovered the Boat Place on the west coast of Kikertak (King William Island). The ship's boat sledge was pointed north, toward the camp at Victory Point and the ice-bound ships, not south toward Konajuk (Great Fish River) where the party is believed to have been headed. Considering the immense weight of the sledge and the effort involved in moving it across the island, most researchers have been confused and at a loss for any reason for the sledge to be oriented in that direction. Woodman uses this detail as one of the most convincing pieces of the puzzle in making the case for his alternative reconstruction of events. If a party of 40 men was trekking south for Konajuk (Great Fish River), and the total crew had broken up into multiple parties taking different routes, the ship's boat at the Boat Place could be the remains of a supportive work detail, making a run back to fetch supplies for the larger group. If it was running low on food, the commander of the larger party may have sent a small crew of his healthiest men on a supply run.

It is well within the realm of possibility that a Royal Navy party, weakened by scurvy and on the brink of starvation, would dispatch a smaller group of strong men to return to the ships or the camp at Victory Point where additional canned food supplies may have been located. It has also been observed on various expeditions that small caches of canned food had been placed along the route that the larger party followed (Woodman, 2015), and this is characteristic of the sort of planning one might expect. With the prominence of advanced scurvy observed on many of the skeletal remains recovered from Kikertak (King William Island) (Beattie & Geiger, 1989), the picture becomes more clear. The Expedition was becoming very sick due to the lack of vitamin C in their diets, and while the Royal Navy had several methods for fending off scurvy, it was a problem they were not equipped to deal with once it became especially prominent. Ascorbic acid (vitamin C) is an unstable molecule that degrades over time, so preserved foods and bottled lemon juice are only effective sources of the nutrient for a limited period (DeSantis, 1993).

The Franklin Expedition does not appear to have been facing starvation in early 1848, but the problem of scurvy would have created a desperate scenario demanding the sort of urgent action seen in their attempted long march to the south. The only available remedy to scurvy was large quantities of fresh food, most plants and animals are capable of producing their own vitamin C, so humans rely on dietary sources to access it (DeSantis, 1993). From previous expeditions, likely George Back's account of his descent of the Konajuk (Great Fish River) from 1833-35, they would have known that the area around the mouth of Konajuk (Great Fish River) was a key bottleneck for the annual migration of caribou. Back described herds of caribou so vast and dense as to make hunting them difficult because it was impossible to pick out a target (Woodman, 2015). Copies of Back's account were contained in the libraries of *Erebus* and *Terror*, and it is easy to assume that Crozier and Fitzjames would have looked at the accounts of all expeditions that had explored the vicinity of Kikertak (King William Island).

If the expedition found it necessary to make the long trek to Konajuk (Great Fish River) with their sickest men, it would make sense for them to lay out supplies in advance. These small caches of canned food could have been placed along the coast for them to pick up and reduce the overall weight of the sledges, and it looks like a reasonably well-planned mission one might expect these capable officers to put together.

This version of events also explains why the party was headed to Konajuk (Great Fish River) instead of Fury Beach. Members of the crew were well aware of stores of food left over at that location, Captain Crozier had been present on the expedition that stacked those supplies when *Fury* was abandoned, and Thomas Blanky, ice master on *Terror*, was a part of the crew of Ross's private expedition with *Victory*, and had been saved by those supplies once before (Woodman, 2015). Blanky would have been well aware of how much food was left behind and the condition of it. Furthermore, all of the officers would have been aware of the geography, and that Fury Beach was a good place to affect a rescue. Search expeditions would almost certainly stop there, but even if they didn't it was within striking distance of the whaling fleet. So why not go to Fury Beach? What if Crozier and Fitzjames were not primarily concerned with starvation? If the more pressing concern was scurvy and malnutrition, 30 year old canned food similar to what they already had access to would not solve the problem. If fresh meat was the solution they were in search of, Back's account of the caribou migration at Konajuk (Great Fish River) could appear to be the most reasonable solution.

In the standard reconstruction of events, it is assumed that the party was headed to Konajuk (Great Fish River) to escape. They were planning to paddle upriver to the HBC outpost. The mental state of the officers is generally questioned at this point, because this is by far the most difficult escape option available to the crew. For one thing, once they reach the mouth of the river, the survivors are still over 1,000 kilometers away as the crow flies to the nearest HBC outpost. Moreover, the Konajuk (Great Fish River) was well established as being the most difficult of the three great rivers in the Inuit Nunangat to travel, with more than 80 rapids and waterfalls that would need to be portaged around. It is a challenging and dangerous river for healthy and well-equipped expeditions, but for weakened, sick men without the right boats for river travel? The plan appears suicidal. Many researchers have dismissed this poor decision making as a symptom of lead poisoning and general mental decline (Brandt, 2010).

Woodman's (2015) account makes the case that they were not trying to escape via Konajuk (Great Fish River) at all. Their primary focus could easily have been on solving the problem of scurvy and they may therefore have been travelling to the one place within reach that was a viable solution. After reaching the river and spending a few months hunting and regaining their strength, they could review their options. One option being to traverse north to Fury Beach and launch into Tallurutiup Imanga (Lancaster Sound), as Ross had done in 1833 to affect rescue. Had they survived the trek to Konajuk (Great Fish River) this plan would almost certainly have worked, considering that nearly all search attempts travelled through Tallurutiup Imanga (Lancaster Sound), a large number of them went to Fury Beach, and even if the survivors were not picked up by search expeditions the whaling fleet regularly probed that region as well. Or they could travel west along the coast to the Coppermine River, which is much more easily navigated than the Konajuk (Great Fish River), and used that to access either Great Bear Lake or Great Slave Lake where they could find shelter with the HBC. Several overland expeditions were present in that part of the Inuit Nunangat as well, most of which left behind caches of food for Franklin's men to find. A benefit to Woodman's (2015) reconstruction is that it is supported by the Inuit testimony. In the various encounters described by the Netsilik, the kabloona leader, Aglooka, always tells them they are headed to the Konajuk (Great Fish River) to hunt deer. None of these accounts claims he was headed there to escape or return home. This can be chalked up to the poor quality of communication between the kabloonas and the Netsilik since none spoke each others language very well, but it is also supported by the fact that in the margin note on the Victory Point document, Crozier merely wrote that they were headed to Konajuk (Great Fish River) the following day. The brevity of this note is characteristic of Royal Navy communications, but it does not offer any explanation of what they planned to do at Konajuk (Great Fish River). It has been left up to interpretation whether Crozier intended to escape there, or simply to hunt.

Also important is the artifacts found at the camp at Victory Point near the cairn. McClintock describes a camp filled with useless articles that make no sense to bring ashore for an escape mission (Brandt, 2010). Again the traditional narrative chalks this up to the same cause of the illogical plan to paddle up Konajuk (Great Fish River): the crew must have been suffering from poor mental health. But Woodman (2015) digs deeper into the account of the Victory Point camp to draw some interesting conclusions. It appears as though the camp had been in operation for a long period of time, beyond being the rallying point for the long march south. It appears the camp was used as the staging area to support the scientific and exploratory parties of the expedition soon after they were locked into the ice, a sensible location being as it was the closest land to where the ships were trapped. One detail commonly fixated on is the pile of clothing four feet high observed by McClintock, with worn out tent canvas on the ground nearby. McClintock and his men combed through every scrap of clothing in the pile and found no personal items or notes at all. The condition of the clothing when it was deposited was difficult to deduce since after ten years exposed to the elements the fabric was badly rotted. Woodman speculates that the clothing had been neatly stacked in that spot and covered with a tent because the location was intended to remain a supply depot, he argues the crew planned to return to that location after their hunting expedition to the south. It makes sense that the canvas tent found near the pile of clothing could have been placed over it to shelter the pile from the elements in the summer months, but not as a long-term solution. The first winter storm, Woodman (2015) argues, would shred the tent. But if the party was planning a return near the start of winter, however, it would be reasonable to stockpile their warm clothing at a centralized location instead of hauling the items with them through the summer. The Netsilik use a similar method for storing their winter clothing and equipment during the summer months to avoid the needless burning of calories hauling useless items for their summer activities (Balikci, 1989). If the party was planning to return to the site at a later time, items such as the medicine chest, pile of clothing, iron rings, hollow curtain rods, food stores, and other assorted items found at Victory Point appear less frivolous.

It is not possible to truly know what occurred in those final weeks of the Expedition, but Woodman (2015) makes some interesting points that offer reasonable explanations for some of the more bizarre elements of this story. Either way, Crozier and Fitzjames were throwing a figurative hail-mary to save their sick and dying crew.

Summary

Researchers have conducted an extensive amount of study into the Franklin Expedition in an effort to illuminate the complicated factors leading to the disaster. This chapter has reviewed a handful of them, but much more has been conducted and more still is currently underway. The aim of this chapter has been to shed light on some of the current theories and arguments about the role that various factors played in the decisions made by the officers in charge, and the ultimate outcomes of the Expedition. From Woodman's theory that the crew was going to Konajuk (Great Fish River) to obtain fresh meat with the intention of regrouping and affecting their escape later, to the debate over malnutrition, botulism, and lead poisoning. The crew of the Franklin Expedition faced a wealth of threats from all sides, including those mentioned above but not to the exclusion of the risks posed by the ice pack, extreme temperatures, wildlife, and the more universal risks associated with service aboard a sailing ship.

The details of what happened in the final weeks and months of the expedition are apparent thanks to the dedicated efforts of researchers and explorers spanning more than a century. Questions about lead poisoning, zinc deficiency, scurvy, and tuberculosis in combination with what little is known of the deaths experienced up until the magin note on the Victory Point document paint a picture of a miserable situation long before the ships were abandoned (Brandt, 2010; Beattie & Geiger, 1989; Woodman, 2015; Christensen et al, 2017). The choice to haul heavy sledges across the punishing terrain of Kikertak (King William Island) leaves us with images of the suffering endured after Crozier and Fitzjames made the decision to leave the ships. And the final efforts to survive culminating in cannibalism between crewmates (Beattie & Geiger, 1989; Mays & Beattie, 2016) gives a last glimpse into just how desperate the situation became and the lengths to which the final survivors were pushed in their quest to escape.

The story of Franklin's final expedition is complicated. Often it is presented in simplistic terms with much of the nuance stripped away. When researching this topic, the distances and locations are challenging to comprehend, but when following along on a map it becomes much clearer. While ice is the primary factor in whether expeditions succeeded or failed, it is important to see just how parties could travel on foot across land and sea ice. So much focus is placed on the ships but in truth most of the mapping was done on a much smaller scale. Sledge parties sent out by Parry and the two Ross's covered unthinkable distances. Franklin, Back, Richardson, Rae, Hall, and Schwatka traversed challenging terrain to varying degrees of success but all of them travelled distances that are startling to contemporary sensibilities. This story cannot be properly told without attempting to appreciate the successes and failures of earlier expeditions. Debate over the actions taken by Franklin, Crozier, and Fitzjames during the expedition, or later by the search parties is incomplete without establishing the proper context for what resources existed in the region and what areas were most easily accessed by vessels. This body of knowledge creates a far more illuminating picture of the events.

Conclusion

It is also important to recognize the traditions and knowledge of the Inuit, and the Netsilik in particular, because they have preserved accounts of the final days of the expedition that are often ignored. They also set the table to understand what practices are necessary to travel and survive in the Inuit Nunangat; that foundation of knowledge creates an interesting lens through which to view the Franklin Expedition, because one can easily identify a great many points of failure in the methodology employed. They were simply not adapted to travel through the region. The shocking result of having a 100% fatality rate was not a foregone conclusion from the outset, but events certainly conspired against Franklin at every turn and his own apparent disregard for hazards made Franklin a lucky man for having survived his first overland expedition, and a dead man on his third attempt to lead a crew in the Inuit Nunangat.

Focus tends to land on Franklin's men but it is important to recognize the impacts on the Indigenous population as well, conceivably by destabilizing the food chain on Kikertak (King William Island) and creating a sudden influx of rare raw materials such as wood and iron (Balikci, 1989; Brandt, 2010; Thacher, 2018). It was also the culmination of decades of Royal Navy efforts to navigate the Northwest Passage which included dozens of vessels and the efforts of thousands of people. The disappearance of the Expedition inspired a wave of additional expeditions that were sent in search of the lost ships and crew, furthering the impact on Indigenous peoples. These combined efforts inspired the British public for generations and the story of Franklin and his men has inspired interest around the world for nearly two centuries. And whether lead poisoning, zinc deficiency, or scurvy played the primary role in the deaths of all involved, what can be agreed upon easily is that Franklin's men were besieged on all sides by threats. There was perhaps not one single danger they faced that caused their demise, but a storm of factors including illness and malnutrition, but also technological failure, arrogance, and mother nature as well.

It is also a story of the heights of hubris, propelled by a national character of empire and exploration, crushed under the weight of sea ice and a stubborn refusal to learn from Indigenous traditions in one of the most extreme environments on the planet. Moreover, it was well understood by the explorers themselves, the Admiralty, and the British public long before the Franklin Expedition that the Northwest Passage, if it was discovered, would have been far too dangerous and unpredictable to be useful as a trade route to India. The only purpose for the continued effort was the pursuit of national prestige. If there are lessons still to be learned from the Franklin Expedition, hopefully they are in the value of traditional knowledge held by the Indigenous peoples of the region.

Appendix I

List of Northwest Passage Expeditions and Rescue Operations

This is a list given by Brandt (2010). It includes all of the major and many of the minor efforts, but does leave out activities in the region carried out by the whaling fleet, and likely some minor expeditions held by private interests, the Royal Navy, and the United States government as well.

1818	David Buchan, *HMS Dorothea*, and John Franklin, *HMS Trent*
1818	John Ross, *HMS Isabella*, and William Edward Parry, *HMS Alexander*
1819-22	John Franklin, overland
1819-20	William Edward Parry, *HMS Helca*, and Matthew Liddon, *HMS Griper*
1821-23	William Edward Parry, HMS Fury, and George F. Lyon, *HMS Helca*
1824-25	William Edward Parry, *HMS Helca*, and Henry Hoppner, *HMS Fury*
1824	George F. Lyon, *HMS Griper*
1825-27	John Franklin, overland
1825-28	Frederick W. Beechey, *HMS Blossom*

1827	William Edward Parry, *HMS Helca*
1829-33	John Ross, Victory, privately funded
1833-35	George Back, overland
1836-37	George Back, *HMS Terror*
1837-39	Thomas Simpson and Peter Dease, overland
1845-48	John Franklin, *HMS Erebus*, and Francis R.M. Crozier, *HMS Terror*
1846-47	John Rae, overland
1848-49	James Ross, *HMS Enterprise*, and Edward Bird, *HMS Investigator*
1848-52	Thomas Moore, *HMS Plover*
1848-50	John Richardson and John Rae, overland
1848-50	Henry Kellett, *HMS Herald*
1849	Robert Shedden, *Nancy Dawson*, privately funded
1849-51	William J.S. Pullen and W.H. Hooper, small boat following northern coast
1849-50	James Saunders, *HMS North Star*
1850	Charles Forsyth, *Prince Albert*, privately funded by Lady Jane Franklin
1850-51	H.T. Austin, *HMS Resolute*, Erasmus Ommanney, *HMS Assistance*, John Cator, *HMS Intrepid*, Sherard Osborn, *HMS Pioneer*
1850-51	William Penny, *Lady Franklin*, and Alexander Stewart, *Sophia*, privately funded by Lady Jane Franklin

1850-51	John Ross, *Felix*, and yacht *Mary*, privately funded
1850-51	Edwin De Haven, *Advance*, and Samuel Griffin, *Rescue*, privately funded
1850-51	John Rae, by dog sled and small boat
1850-54	Robert McClure, *HMS Investigator*
1850-55	Richard Collinson, *HMS Enterprise*
1851-52	William Kennedy, *Prince Albert*, privately funded by Lady Jane Franklin
1852	Edward Inglefield, *Isabel*, privately funded by Lady Jane Franklin
1852-54	Edward Belcher, *HMS Assistance*, Sherard Osborn, *HMS Pioneer*, Henry Kellett, *HMS Resolute*, and Francis L. McClintock, *HMS Intrepid*
1852-54	William J.S. Pullen, *HMS North Star*
1853-54	John Rae, overland
1855	James Anderson, overland
1857-59	Francis L. McClintock, *Fox*, privately funded by Lady Jane Franklin
1864-69	Charles Francis Hall, overland
1878-80	Frederick Schwatka, overland

Appendix II
Crew List *HMS Erebus* & *HMS Terror*

These lists are taken from the muster books of *HMS Erebus* and *HMS Terror*, 1845. Taken from Admiralty Records, Public Record Office.

HMS Erebus

Captain Sir John Franklin

Commander James Fitzjames

Lieutenants Graham Gore, H.T.D. Le Vesconte, James W. Fairholme

Mates Robert O. Sargent, Charles F. Des Voeux, Edward Couch

Second Master Henry F. Collins

Surgeon Stephen S. Stanley

Acting Assistant-Surgeon Harry D.S. Goodsir

Paymaster and Purser Charles H. Osmer

Acting Master James Reid

Warrant Officers John Gregory (engineer), Thomas Terry (boatswain), John Weekes (carpenter)

Petty Officers Phillip Reddington (captain of the forecastle), Thomas Watson (carpenter's mate), John Murray (sailmaker), James W. Brown (caulker), William Smith (blacksmith), Samuel Brown (boatswain's mate), Richard Wall (cook), James Rigden (captain's coxswain), John Sullivan (captain of the maintop), Robert Sinclair (captain of the foretop), Joseph Andrews (captain of the hold) Edmund Hoar (captain's steward), Richard Aylmore (gunroom steward), Daniel Arthur (quartermaster), John Downing (quartermaster) William Bell (quartermaster), Francis Dunn (caulker's mate), William Fowler (paymaster and purser's steward), John Bridgens (subordinate officer's steward), James Hart (leading stoker), John Cowie (stoker), Thomas Plater (stoker)

Able Seamen Henry Lloyd, John Stickland, Thomas Hartnell, John Hartnell, George Thompson, William Orren, Charles Coombs, William Closson, William Mark, Thomas Work, Charles Best, George Williams, John Morfin, Thomas Tadman, Abraham Seely, Thomas McConvey, Robert Ferrier, Josephus Geater, Robert Johns, Francis Pocock

Royal Marines David Bryant (sergeant), Alexander Paterson (corporal), Joseph Healey (private), William Braine (private), William Reed (private), Robert Hopcraft (private), William Pilkington (private)

Boys George Chambers, David Young

HMS Terror

Captain Francis Rawdon Moira Crozier

Lieutenants Edward Little, John Irving, George H. Hodgson

Mates Robert Thomas, Frederick John Hornby

Second Master Gillies A. Macbean

Surgeon John S. Peddie

Assistant Surgeon Alexander MacDonald

Clerk-In-Charge E.J.H. Helpman

Acting Master Thomas Blanky

Warrant Officers Thomas Honey (carpenter), John Lane (boatswain), James Thompson (engineer)

Petty Officers Reuben Male (captain of the forecastle), Thomas Johnson (boatswain's mate), John Torrington (leading stoker) Alexander Wilson (carpenter's mate), David MacDonald (quartermaster), William Rhodes (quartermaster), John Kenley (quartermaster), Thomas Darlington (caulker), John Diggle (cook), Thomas Farr (captain of the maintop), Henry Peglar (captain of the foretop), John Wilson (captain's coxswain), Samuel Honey (blacksmith), William Goddard (captain of the hold), Thomas Jopson (captain's steward), Thomas Armitage (gunroom steward), Cornelius Hickey (caulker's mate), Edward Genge (paymaster's steward), William Gibson (subordinate officer's steward), Luke Smith (stoker), William Johnson (stoker)

Able Seamen George Cann, William Shanks, David Sims, William Sinclair, William Jerry, Henry Sait, Alexander Berry, John Bailey, Samuel Crispe, John Bates, William Wentzall, William Strong, John Handford, Charles Johnson, David Leys, George Kinnaird, Magnus Manson, James Walker, Edwin Laurence

Royal Marines Solomon Tozer (sergeant), William Hedges (corporal), Henry Wilks (private), John Hammond (private), James Daly (private), William Heather (private)

Boys Robert Golding, Thomas Evans

Appendix III Inuit Nunangat Map

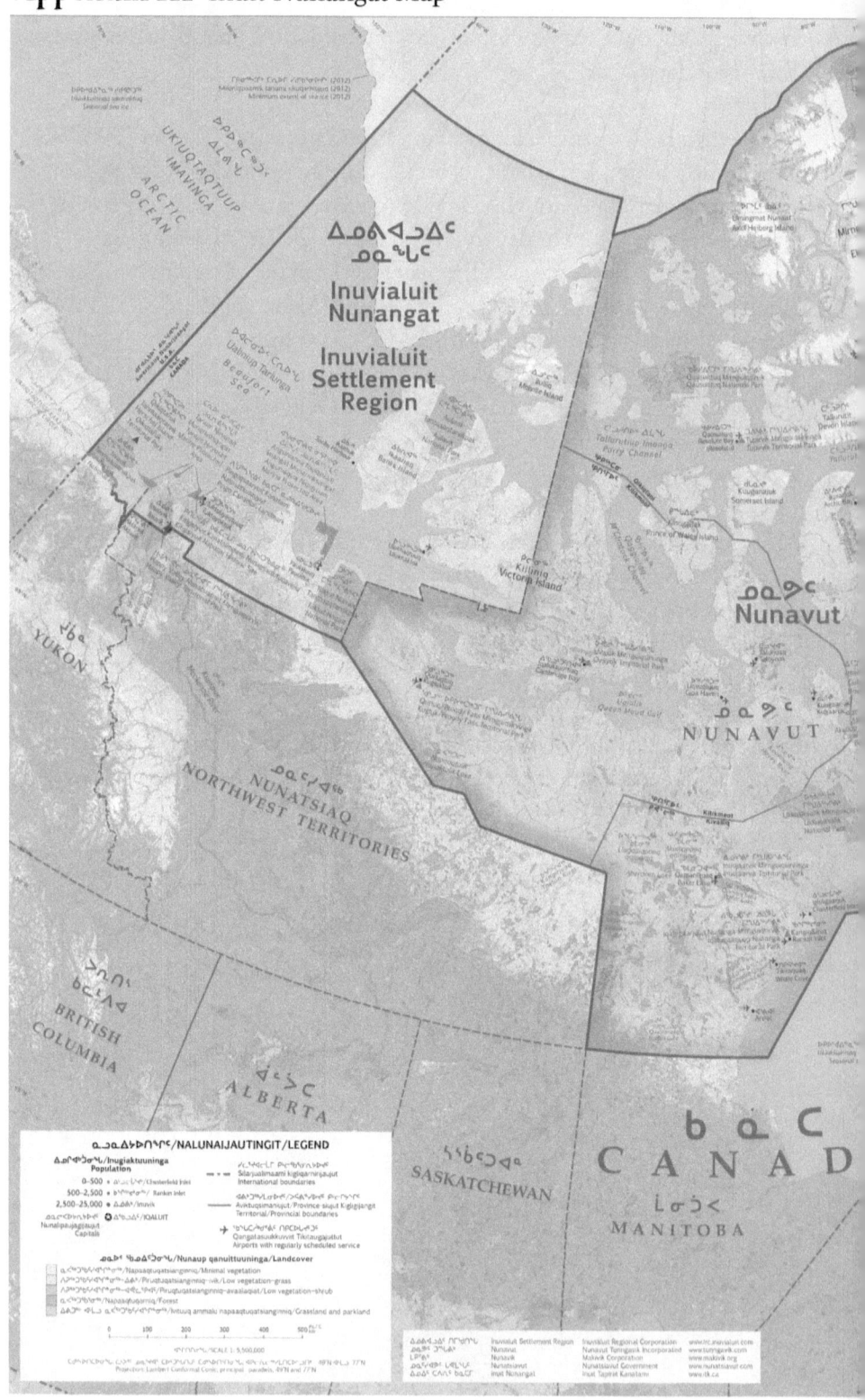

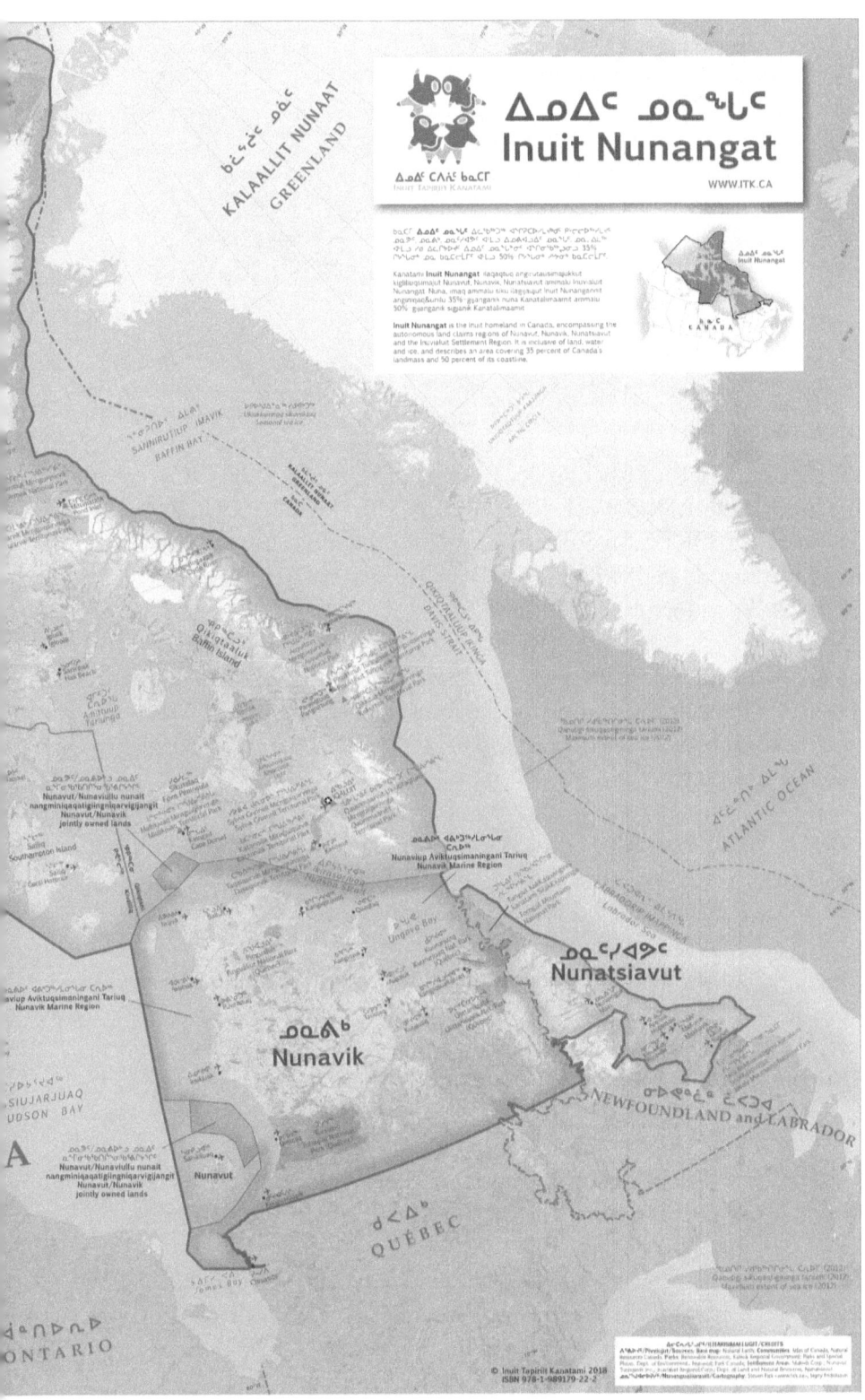

Source: Inuit Tapiriit Kanatami, 2018 (modified/altered).

References

Alt, B., Koerner, R., Fisher, D., & Bourgeois, J. (1985). ARCTIC CLIMATE DURING THE FRANKLIN ERA, AS DEDUCED FROM ICE CORES. In Sutherland P. (Ed.), Franklin Era in Canadian Arctic History, 1845-1859 (pp. 69-92). University of Ottawa Press. doi:10.2307/j.ctv16pgd.11

Appelt, M., Jensen, J. F., Myrup, M., Haack, H., Sørensen, M., & Taube, M. (2014). The cultural History of the Innaanganeq/Cape York Meteorite. Nunatta Katersugaasivia Allagaateqarfialu / The Greenland National Museum & Archives.

Back, G. (1836). Narrative of the Arctic land expedition to the mouth of the Great Fish River: And along the shores of the Arctic Ocean, in the years 1833, 1834 and 1835. London: J. Murray.

Balikci, A. (1989). The Netsilik Eskimo. Prospect Heights, IL: Waveland Press.
Barr, W. (2009). The Use of Dog Sledges during the British Search for the Missing Franklin Expedition in the North American Arctic Islands, 1848-59. Arctic, 62(3), 257–272.

Beattie, O., & Geiger, J. (1989). Frozen in time: Unlocking the secrets of the Franklin Expedition. Saskatoon: Western Producer Prairie Books.

Brandt, A. (2010). The Man Who Ate His Boots: Sir John Franklin and the Tragic History of the Northwest Passage. New York: Alfred A. Knopf.
Britannica.com. (n.d.). Sir John Franklin. Retrieved August 29, 2021, from https://www.britannica.com/biography/John-Franklin

Byard, R. W. (2021). Death in the Arctic - the tragic fate of members of the Franklin expedition (1845). Forensic Science, Medicine, and Pathology, 17(1), 161. https://doi.org/10.1007/s12024-020-00305-5

Christensen, J. R., McBeth, J. M., Sylvain, N. J., Spence, J., & Chan, H. M. (2017). Hartnell's time machine: 170-year-old nails reveal severe zinc deficiency played a greater role than lead in the demise of the Franklin Expedition. Journal of Archaeological Science: Reports, 16, 430–440. https://doi.org/10.1016/j.jasrep.2016.11.042

Crozier, F., Capt. (1845, July 9). Francis Crozier Letter to James Ross [Letter to James Ross]. Whalefish Islands, Greenland.

Dease, P. W., & Barr, W. (2002). From Barrow to Boothia: The Arctic journal of Chief Factor Peter Warren Dease, 1836-1839. Montreal: McGill-Queens University Press.

Desantis, J. (1993). Scurvy and Psychiatric Symptoms. Perspectives in Psychiatric Care, 29(1), 18-22. doi:10.1111/j.1744-6163.1993.tb00397.x

Fitzpatrick, K. (1949). Sir John Franklin in Tasmania, 1837-1843. Melbourne: Melbourne University Press.

Forst J, & Brown T.A. (2017). A Case Study : Was Private William Braine of the 1845 Franklin Expedition a Victim of Tuberculosis? Arctic, 70(4), 381–388.

Franklin, J. S. (1823). Narrative of a journey to the shores of the Polar Sea in the years 1819, 20, 21, and 22. Edmonton: Reprint: MG Hurtig, 1969.

Franklin, J. (1845a). Sir John Franklin Letter to Isabella Cracroft [Letter to Isabella Cracroft]. 21 Bedford Place, London.

Franklin, J. (1845b). Sir John Franklin Letter to Lady Jane Franklin [Letter to Lady Jane Franklin]. 40 Lower Brook Street, Ipswich.

Franklin, J. (1845c). Sir John Franklin Letter to Sir William Parry [Letter to Sir William Parry]. Whale Fish Island, Greenland.

Franklin, J. (1983). Narrative of a second expedition to the shores of the Polar Sea: In the years 1825, 1826, and 1827. 1828. Zug: Inter Documentation.

Franklin, J. S. (1995). Sir John Franklin's journals and correspondence: The first arctic land expedition, 1819-1822 (R. C. Davis, Ed.). Toronto: The Champlain Society.

Hood, R., & Houston, C. S. (1974). To the Arctic by canoe 1819-1821 ; the journal and paintings of Robert Hood, midshipman with Franklin. Montreal: The Arctic Inst. of North America.

Houston, C., & Hochbaum, H. (2014). Arctic Ordeal: The Journal of John Richardson, Surgeon-Naturalist with Franklin, 1820-1822. Montréal: McGill-Queens University Press.

Irving, J. (1845, April 18). Lieutenant Irving Letter to His Sister-in-Law [Letter to Katie]. HMS Terror, Woolwich.

Kaalund, N. K. L. (2020). What Happened to John Franklin? Danish and British Perspectives from Francis McClintock's Arctic Expedition, 1857–59. Journal of Victorian Culture, 25(2), 300–314.

LABARGE, C. (2019). How Two Sunken Ships Caused a War: The Legal and Cultural Battle Between Great Britain, Canada, and the Inuit over the Franklin Expedition Shipwrecks. Loyola of Los Angeles International & Comparative Law Review, 42(1), 79–116.

Markham, C. R. (1909). Life of Admiral Sir Leopold McClintock, K.C.B., D.C.L., LL. D., F.R.S., U.P.R.G.S. London: J. Murray.

Mays, S., & Beattie, O. (2016). Evidence for End-stage Cannibalism on Sir John Franklin's Last Expedition to the Arctic, 1845. International Journal of Osteoarchaeology, 26(5), 778. https://doi.org/10.1002/oa.2479

Moxon, J. (1627–1700). (2017). Oxford Dictionary of National Biography. doi:10.1093/odnb/9780192683120.013.19466

O'Dochartaigh, E. (2019). "Exceedingly Good Friends:" The Representation of Indigenous People during the Franklin Search Expeditions to the Arctic, 1847-59. Victorian Studies, 61(2), 255. https://doi.org/10.2979/victorianstudies.61.2.10

Online Etymology Dictionary. (n.d.). Erebus: Search Online Etymology Dictionary. Retrieved September 05, 2021, from https://www.etymonline.com/search?q=erebus

Parry, W. E. (1821). Journal of a voyage for the discovery of a Northwest Passage from the Atlantic to the Pacific: Performed in the years 1819-20, in Her Majestys ships Hecla and Griper .. London: John Murray.

Parry, W. E. (1824). Journal of a second voyage for the discovery of a north-west passage from the Atlantic to the Pacific: Performed in the years 1821-22-23, in His Majestys ships Fury and Hecla, under the orders of Captain William Edward Parry, R.N., F.R.S., and commander of the expedition. London: J. Murray.

Parry, W. E. (1826). Journal of a third voyage for the discovery of a North-West passage: From the Atlantic to the Pacific: Performed in the years 1824-25, in His Majestys ships Hecla and Fury. London: John Murray.

Potter, R. (2019, April 10). Tasting "Tripe de Roche" at Mystic. Retrieved August 01, 2021, from https://visionsnorth.blogspot.com/2019/04/tasting-tripe-de-roche-at-mystic.html

Rae, J. (1953). John Raes correspondence with the Hudsons Bay Company on Arctic exploration. London: Hudsons Bay Record Society.

Richardson, J. (1851). Arctic searching expedition. London: Longman, Brown, Green and Longmans.

Ross, J. (1819). A voyage of discovery: Made under the orders of the Admiralty, in His Majestys ships Isabella and Alexander, for the purpose of exploring Baffins Bay, and enquiring into the probability of a north-west passage. London: John Murray.

Ross, M. J. (1994). Polar Pioneers: John Ross and James Clark Ross. Montreal: McGill-Queens University Press.

Stenton, D. R., & Park, R. W. (2020). The "Cast Iron Site"--A Tale of Four Stoves from the 1845 Franklin Northwest Passage Expedition. Arctic, 73(1), 1–12. https://doi.org/10.14430/arctic69830

Houston C.S. (2007). Captain Francis Crozier: Last Man Standing? Michael Smith. Arctic, 60(2), 206–207.

Smith, M. (2014). Captain Francis Crozier: Last man standing? Cork: The Collins Press.

Taichman, R. S., Gross, T., & MacEachern, M. P. (2017). A Critical

Assessment of the Oral Condition of the Crew of the Franklin Expedition. Arctic, 70(1), 25–36. https://doi.org/10.14430/arctic4629

Thacher, D. (2018). Salvaging on the Coast of Erebus Bay, King William Island : An Analysis of Inuit Interaction with Material from the Franklin Expedition. Arctic, 71(4), 431–443.

Traill, H. D. (1896). The life of Sir John Franklin, R.N. With maps, portraits, and facsimiles. London.

Williams, G. (2003). Voyages of delusion: The search for the Northwest Passage in the Age of Reason. London: HarperCollins.

Woodman, D. C. (2015). Unravelling the Franklin mystery: Inuit testimony. Montreal: McGill-Queens Univ. Press.

Woodward, F. J. (1951). Portrait of Jane: A life of Lady Franklin. London: H. & S.

www.ingramcontent.com/pod-product-compliance
Lightning Source LLC
Chambersburg PA
CBHW021915180426
43198CB00035B/662